I0582904

the sweet life

101 indulgent recipes with less sugar

the sweet life

101 indulgent recipes with less sugar

antony worrall thompson

photography by steve baxter

kyle cathie ltd

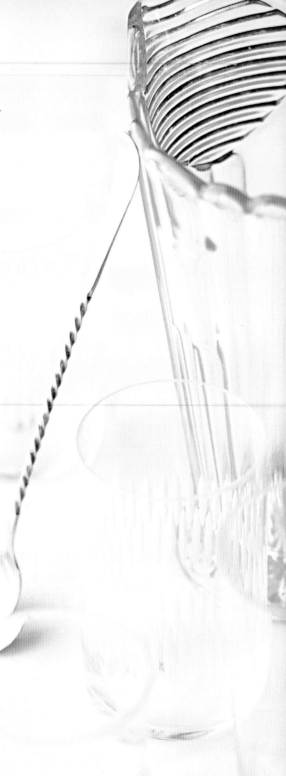

Acknowledgements

To my wife Jacinta and our children Toby and Billie who helped me with the enjoyable task of trying all the recipes in this book.

To the team at Splenda with whom I have worked closely for many years now, developing delicious recipes, without the sugar. To the team at Hill & Knowlton for their help in making this book a success.

To Sue Ashworth and Joanna Farrow who tested the recipes and worked their way through many boxes of Splenda in the process! To Steve Baxter, his assistant Delphine Bodart and props stylist Rachel Jukes for the beautiful images. To my publisher, Kyle Cathie, for taking on this exciting project. To my editor, Suzanna de Jong, and the team at Kyle Cathie Ltd for making this fantastic book in no time at all.

Published in 2008 by
Kyle Cathie Limited
122 Arlington Road, London NW1 7HP
general.enquiries@kyle-cathie.com
www.kylecathie.com

ISBN 978-1-85626-815-8

Text © 2008 Antony Worrall Thompson, except for pp14, 18, 20, 24, 39, 46, 50, 54, 60, 61, 67, 86, 90, 103, 104, 109, 117-132, 135, 136, 142, 146, 150, 156, 159, 160, 164, 167, 168 and 171 © Splenda (McNeil Nutritional Ltd)
Photography © Splenda (McNeil Nutritional Ltd), except for p7 © Alan Strutt and Melinda Messenger, and p9 © Harry Borden
Design © 2008 Kyle Cathie Ltd

All rights reserved. No reproduction, copy or transmission of this publication may be made without written permission. No paragraph of this publication may be reproduced, copied or transmitted save with written permission or in accordance with the provisions of the Copyright Act 1956 (as amended). Any person who does any unauthorised act in relation to this publication may be liable to criminal prosecution and civil claims for damages.

Editor: Suzanna de Jong
Designer: Geoff Hayes
Photographer: Steve Baxter
Home Economist: Sue Ashworth
Prop Stylist: Rachel Jukes
Recipe Analysis: Wendy Doyle
Production: Sha Huxtable

Antony Worrall Thompson is hereby identified as the author of this work in accordance with Section 77 of the Copyright, Designs and Patents Act 1988.

A Cataloguing in Publication record for this title is available from the British Library.

Colour reproduction by Sang Choy
Printed and bound in China by C&C Offset

contents

foreword

Calling all dessert lovers!

A balanced diet and regular exercise are important aspects of my life, making me feel healthier and helping me to stay in shape. But as a busy Mum with three kids, my days are hectic and the gym is often a distant memory, so meal times become my main focus.

Meal times give me a chance to catch up with the kids on all the excitement of the day while making sure we've all had a healthy, nutritious meal. And guess what? That doesn't mean all desserts go out of the window! So what's my secret to delicious, homemade desserts that I'm happy for all the family to enjoy? Well, it's all thanks to Antony Worrall Thompson.

I've known Antony for several years and have always adored his cooking, so I've often asked him for tips and advice. The best tip he's ever given me is to substitute sugar for Splenda sweetener where I can. It's the perfect way to make hundreds of yummy desserts without all the calories of sugar. By taking his advice, I can make lighter desserts that are better for my waistline and healthier for my family, but still taste great.

When it comes to weekends, my kitchen is always buzzing. The whole family piles in and the kids always insist that we bake together. Despite the mess, this is my favourite way to spend the day and we've tried lots of sweet recipes using Splenda instead of sugar. The kids can't even tell the difference.

Providing I've got the time, I can also be pretty adventurous in the kitchen if I'm entertaining. When dessert is on the menu and my friends find out that they've been made with sweetener instead of sugar, guess who's the popular one!

I was delighted when Antony asked me to contribute eight of my favourite recipes to this book. The recipes that I've chosen are favourites with me, my friends and, most importantly, my kids. Ranging from an everyday Rice Pudding and tasty Chocolate Brownies, to a delicious Tiramisù and Christmas Punch, they are all low in sugar and so simple to make.

So go on, what are you waiting for, get cooking and enjoy these delicious treats!

Love,
Melinda Messenger

introduction

Baking and making your own puddings seems to be a dying practice in many homes these days – what a shame. I have fond childhood memories of sitting around the table as a family, eating a homemade cake or dessert. It was such a treat, and I feel that, actually, all of us should get to enjoy a bit of sweetness now and again, after dinner or as a snack.

Unfortunately, children spend a lot of their time sitting down nowadays, in front of the TV, at the computer or with a Game Boy. Adults aren't much better really, using the car for errands and shopping and claiming we're too busy to go to the gym. The fact is we don't get nearly enough exercise and this makes it hard to sustain a healthy, old-fashioned diet.

Obesity is a growing problem in adults and children alike, and something our generation needs to deal with. It's vital to our health that we find ways to reduce our daily calorific intake, but at the same time, it is equally important that we continue to enjoy the food we eat! Food is not just about health, and it's not about excluding any particular food groups or ingredients. It's all about balance.

Sugar as a food group is one that you can easily cut back on in my opinion. Sugar gives you energy, but our bodies can get all the energy they need from other carbohydrates as well, so you don't need to consume that much sugar at all. But, and this is a big but, many of us thoroughly enjoy sweet things, and we mustn't deny ourselves those sweet cravings. Enter Splenda. By replacing some, if not most, of the sugar you add to your food with Splenda, you can reduce the calorie intake of your family.

I started using Splenda myself when I found out I was heading towards diabetes. My resistance to insulin, a hormone that helps the body to process sugar and use it as fuel, was so high that I was at risk of developing diabetes. I had to take drastic steps to reduce my weight. But, as a chef, I want to cook my family the food that they love to eat. By using Splenda, I have managed to do both – reduce the amount of sugar I eat while still cooking delicious things.

The fantastic thing about Splenda, giving it the thumbs up over some other sweeteners on the market, is that it can be used in cooking and baking. I've tried many different sweeteners over the years, only to become frustrated. While perfectly suitable to stir into your tea and coffee, or to sprinkle over your cereal, I couldn't use them for the thing I like best: cooking.

The recipes in this book full of sweet things use Splenda sweetener rather than sugar where possible. This doesn't mean there's no sugar in them at all – I've still used ingredients that contain natural sugars such as fruit, and some of the baking recipes need a little bit of sugar, honey or syrup to make them work. However, the sugar content has been cut down as much as possible for each and every recipe and, remember, when it comes to controlling your weight, every little helps. If you have diabetes, you'll know through your doctor or nutritionist what you can and cannot eat. I've added nutritional information at the end of each recipe to help you make the right choice for you.

So here's to enjoying sweetness again – as part of a healthy, balanced lifestyle.

all about Splenda

What is Splenda?

If you're looking to reduce the amount of sugar in your diet without compromising on taste, then there is an easy way: with SPLENDA® Low Calorie Sweetener. Splenda is the only sweetener on the market that is made with sucralose, a unique ingredient that is made from sugar and tastes like sugar but without all the calories.

Available in granulated and tablet form, Splenda can be used as a tasty alternative to sugar. Unlike some other sweeteners, Splenda is heat stable and keeps its delicious sweet taste at high temperatures, making it the perfect alternative to sugar when cooking and baking.

You can use Splenda spoon for spoon like sugar and reduce the number of calories you consume – Splenda has only 2 calories per teaspoon, where sugar has 20 calories per teaspoon.

Splenda and diabetes

Splenda is suitable for people with diabetes to use as part of a healthy, balanced diet. Sucralose, the sweetening ingredient in Splenda, is not metabolised by the body. As a result, Splenda has an insignificant effect on insulin or blood glucose levels. This means that by replacing sugar with Splenda, even people with diabetes can enjoy sweet dishes and baked treats.

Tips for cooking and baking with Splenda

When cooking and baking, it is useful to keep in mind that Splenda works best in recipes where sugar is used to provide a sweet taste, like in pie fillings, sweet sauces and glazes. Try replacing every 100g of sugar with about 8 tablespoons of Splenda. It's a good idea to start with a little less Splenda and taste the dish as you go, to see how sweet you like it. For cooking and baking with Splenda, just follow the guidelines below to get great results, without all the calories.

Mixing

There are three ways to successfully incorporate Splenda into a recipe:

❉ Combine thoroughly with other dry ingredients
❉ Dissolve in liquid
❉ Cream with butter or other fat

Sifting

Splenda does not sift like sugar, so if a recipe calls for sifting the dry ingredients, measure the amount of sweetener you need and add it to the other ingredients after sifting.

Creaming

Often when you're baking, the recipe calls for creaming ingredients, such as butter, sweetener and eggs, together. With Splenda, you may need to beat the ingredients a little longer to get enough air into the mixture – that way you'll end up with a more fluffy and even texture.

Cooking

Check your baked goodies 7 to 10 minutes before the end of the suggested cooking time (1 to 2 minutes for biscuits) as some products cook more quickly with Splenda. To make sure a cake is cooked on the inside, just insert a skewer into the middle of the cake – it should come out clean. If it's still sticky, cook it for a little longer.

Storing

Products made with Splenda may not last as long as products made with sugar, since sugar acts as a preservative as well as a sweetener. You can make your Splenda products last longer by storing them in airtight containers in the fridge. Most can also be frozen for even longer storage.

For further tips and advice on Splenda visit www.splenda.co.uk

baked treats

summer berry filo slice

SERVES 6

vegetable oil, for greasing
5 large sheets filo pastry
50g butter, melted
300ml double cream
100g raspberries
100g blackberries
2 tablespoons Splenda granulated
    sweetener
100g strawberries, hulled and sliced

This lovely summer dessert uses filo pastry – rather than puff – to make a lighter version of a mille feuille.

Preheat the oven to 200°C/400°F/gas mark 6. Lightly grease 3 baking trays with a little vegetable oil. (If you only have one or two baking trays, you can cook the pastry in batches).

Place one sheet of filo pastry onto a work surface and brush with melted butter. Pile the rest of the filo pastry sheets on top, brushing each separate sheet with melted butter as you go. Use a sharp knife or scissors to cut the pile into three stacks, each measuring approximately 25x12.5cm. Place each stack onto a baking tray.

Bake the filo pastry stacks in the oven for 5–6 minutes, or until golden brown. Remove from the oven and leave to cool completely.

Whip the double cream in a chilled bowl until it forms soft peaks. Crush half the raspberries and blackberries lightly with a fork and add the sweetener. Fold lightly through the cream – there is no need to mix them in thoroughly.

Put one stack of filo pastry sheets onto a serving platter. Spread half the cream mixture over the surface and scatter half the fruit on top. Place another stack of filo pastry on top, then carefully spoon the rest of the cream mixture over. Add the remaining fruit and top with the last stack of filo pastry sheets. Chill until ready to serve.

Per serving: 380kcal; 3g protein; 35g fat; 19.6g saturated fat; 14g carbohydrates; 4.6g sugar; 1.1g fibre; 0.21g sodium

baked cheesecake with marsala steeped raisins

SERVES 10

60g raisins

6 tablespoons marsala

40g unsalted butter, plus extra for
   greasing

125g digestive biscuits, crushed

400g full fat cream cheese

300g natural yogurt

150ml single cream

8 tablespoons Splenda granulated
   sweetener

2 teaspoons vanilla extract

3 eggs, beaten

Unlike many baked cheesecakes, this version is smooth and creamy but not too heavy. The secret of achieving a creamy soft, set centre is to bake it until lightly set around the edges but still very wobbly when you gently shake the tin.

Preheat the oven to 180°C/350°F/gas mark 4. Put the raisins and marsala in a small saucepan and heat until bubbling around the edges. Remove from the heat and leave to stand whilst preparing the cheesecake mixture.

Grease the sides of a 20cm springform cake tin. Melt the butter and mix with the crushed biscuits until they start to bind together. Scoop into the tin and pack down with the back of a spoon.

Using a hand-held electric whisk, beat the cream cheese in a bowl until softened. Add the yogurt, cream, sweetener, vanilla extract, eggs and any unabsorbed marsala from the pan. Beat until smooth. Turn the mixture into the tin and scatter with the raisins.

Bake in the oven for about 35–40 minutes, or until the surface is pale golden and set around the edges but the cake still wobbles when the pan is shaken gently. Loosen the edges with a knife and leave to cool in the tin before transferring to a serving plate.

Per serving: 369kcal; 6g protein; 30g fat; 17.8g saturated fat; 17g carbohydrates; 9.8g sugar; 0.4g fibre; 0.28g sodium

apple and almond puff slices

MAKES 8

butter, for greasing

375g ready-rolled puff pastry, thawed
    if frozen

110g ground almonds

3 tablespoons Splenda granulated
    sweetener

1 egg, beaten

2 eating apples, cored and thinly sliced

25g flaked almonds

These heavenly pastries are simplicity itself to make. Serve them warm with a generous dollop of Greek-style yogurt.

Preheat the oven to 200°C/400°F/gas mark 6. Lightly grease two baking trays.

Unroll the pastry sheet and cut out eight circles using a 9cm cutter. Place four circles onto each baking tray.

Mix the almonds with the sweetener, adding just enough beaten egg to make a fairly stiff paste. Put a tablespoonful of the mixture onto the centre of each pastry circle and spread out a little.

Arrange the apple slices neatly on top of the almond mixture. Brush the pastry with the remaining beaten egg. Sprinkle with the flaked almonds.

Bake in the oven for 12–15 minutes, until the pastries are puffed up and golden brown. Cool for about 10 minutes, then serve warm. The slices are lovely with some Greek-style yogurt.

Per serving: 302kcal; 7g protein; 21g fat; 5.3g saturated fat; 22g carbohydrates; 5.1g sugar; 1.7g fibre; 0.16g sodium

anzac cookies

MAKES 12

115g unsalted butter, cut into cubes, plus extra for greasing

75g wholegrain porridge oats

75g desiccated coconut

100g plain flour

6 tablespoons Splenda granulated sweetener

1 teaspoon bicarbonate of soda

2 teaspoons ground ginger

2 tablespoons golden syrup

These chunky, crumbly cookies are ready to eat in half an hour.

Preheat the oven to 180°C/350°F/gas mark 4. Grease a large baking sheet. Mix the oats, coconut, flour, sweetener, bicarbonate of soda and ginger in a bowl.

Melt the butter with the golden syrup in a small saucepan. Pour the mixture over the dry ingredients and stir together until combined.

Divide the mixture into 12 equal-sized balls. Place onto the baking sheet and flatten, spacing the cookies slightly apart. Bake for 10–12 minutes until slightly risen and golden. Transfer to a wire rack to cool.

Per serving: 173kcal; 2g protein; 12g fat; 8.4g saturated fat; 14g carbohydrates; 3.4g sugar; 1.8g fibre; 0.12g sodium

shortbread

SERVES 8

110g cold butter, cubed, plus extra for greasing

175g plain flour

3 heaped tablespoons Splenda granulated sweetener

1 teaspoon almond essence (optional)

Sue Lancaster won the Splenda Recipe Club competition with this delicious recipe for sugar-free shortbread.

Preheat the oven to 180°C/350°F/gas mark 4. Grease a 20cm baking tin with a little butter. Rub together the flour, butter, sweetener and almond essence, if using, into a dough. Wrap in clingfilm and chill in the fridge for at least 15 minutes. Put the dough into the baking tin and push it to flatten and fill the tin. Prick the dough with a fork and bake for 15–20 minutes until lightly golden. Leave to cool, then serve.

Per serving: 184kcal; 2g protein; 12g fat; 7.5g saturated fat; 18g carbohydrates; 1.1g sugar; 0.7g fibre; 0.09g sodium

plum and marzipan filo tarts

SERVES 6

6 filo pastry sheets, thawed if frozen
100ml delicately flavoured olive oil
100g marzipan, grated
6 large plums, stoned and sliced
4 tablespoons Splenda granulated
  sweetener
Greek-style natural yogurt or whipped
  cream, to serve

These wonderful fruit-filled tarts are equally tasty with sliced apples instead of plums.

Preheat the oven to 190°C/375°F/gas mark 5.

Unfold the filo pastry sheets and lay flat on top of each other. Cut through all six layers to form six squares, each measuring approximately 10x10cm. Layer these filo squares into six individual tartlet tins, brushing each pastry sheet with a little olive oil.

Sprinkle an equal amount of grated marzipan into each pastry case. Toss the sliced plums with the sweetener, then divide them between the cases.

Bake for 10–12 minutes until the plums are tender and the pastry is golden brown. Cool slightly, then serve with yogurt or whipped cream.

Per serving: 303kcal; 3g protein; 18g fat; 2.4g saturated fat; 34g carbohydrates; 20.2g sugar; 1.6g fibre; 0.23g sodium

cheat's baklava

SERVES 8

for the filling:
200g pine nuts
200g soft cheese
½ teaspoon ground cloves
1 tablespoon runny honey
1 teaspoon Splenda granulated
   sweetener

450g filo pastry
melted butter, for brushing
runny honey, for drizzling
50g pine nuts, toasted and chopped

This recipe is from my BBC *Saturday Brunch* show. Making it the traditional Greek way is long and fiddly but this version works well and is easy to do in less than 30 minutes. I love the sugary, spicy flavours of good baklava.

Preheat the oven to 180°C/350°F/gas mark 4. For the filling, mix all the ingredients together in a bowl and set aside.

Unfold the filo pastry and, using a sharp knife, carefully cut into thirds. Take two pieces at a time and fold in half. Brush with melted butter. Keeping the narrow end towards you, take some of the filling and spread it over the pastry, keeping a border free along all sides. Fold the sides in to cover the filling and roll up. Repeat with the remaining pastry and filling.

Place the rolls onto a greased baking sheet and brush generously with butter. Bake for 10–15 minutes or until golden brown. Serve the baklava with a drizzle of honey and the toasted pine nuts scattered on top.

Per serving: 632kcal; 11g protein; 50g fat; 19.3g saturated fat; 39g carbohydrates; 7.3g sugar; 0.6g fibre; 0.73g sodium

macaroons

MAKES 12

1 teaspoon vegetable oil
100g whole blanched almonds
50g desiccated coconut
2 egg whites
½ teaspoon cream of tartar
25g golden caster sugar
3 tablespoons Splenda granulated
   sweetener

When ground almonds are a focal ingredient in a recipe, it's best to use whole blanched almonds and grind them in a food processor to bring out their flavour, though you can use shop-bought ground almonds as a time saver.

Preheat the oven to 180°C/350°F/gas mark 4. Line a large baking sheet with bakin and brush with the oil.

Reserve 12 of the almonds and grind the remainder in a food processor. Add the coconut and blend again until the coconut is partially ground.

Using a hand-held electric whisk, whisk the egg whites in a thoroughly clean bowl until foamy. Add the cream of tartar and whisk again until stiff. Mix together the caster sugar and sweetener and gradually whisk into the egg whites, a teaspoonful at a time.

Tip the ground nuts into the bowl and fold in using a large metal spoon. Place spoonfuls onto the baking sheet, spacing them slightly apart. Place a whole almond on each macaroon and bake for 12–15 minutes until golden. Transfer to a wire rack to cool.

Per serving: 90kcal; 2g protein; 7g fat; 2.6g saturated fat; 3g carbohydrates; 3.2g sugar; 1.2g fibre; 0.07g sodium

fruit, nut and seed bars

MAKES 12

175g butter, plus extra for greasing

175g set honey

6 tablespoons Splenda granulated
sweetener

200g porridge oats

pinch of salt

200g fruit and nut mix (dried apricots,
raisins or sultanas, cashew nuts and
coconut shavings are nice)

50g dried cranberries

75g mixed seeds (like sunflower,
pumpkin and linseeds)

50g desiccated coconut

**These yummy energy bars are just the thing for a mid-morning boost,
and they're a perfect fit for a packed lunch or picnic.**

Preheat the oven to 180°C/350°F/gas 4. Grease a 20cm square baking tin and
line with greaseproof paper, leaving an overhang to make it easier to remove the
bars later.

Melt the butter and honey in a large saucepan over a gentle heat. Bring to the
boil and cook for 2 minutes, stirring constantly. Remove from the heat.

Mix together the sweetener, porridge oats, salt, fruit and nut mix, cranberries,
mixed seeds and coconut. Add to the saucepan and stir together until
thoroughly mixed. Tip into the prepared tin and level the surface with the back of
a spoon.

Bake in the oven for 25–30 minutes until golden brown. Cool for 30 minutes,
then remove from the tin and cut into 12 bars. Cool completely on a wire rack.
Keep in an airtight container, or wrap in greaseproof paper.

Per serving: 337kcal; 6g protein; 19g fat; 10.6g saturated fat; 37g carbohydrates;
17.3g sugar; 4.8g fibre; 0.16g sodium

date, walnut and lemon cookies

MAKES 14

75g lightly salted butter, cut into cubes,
   plus extra for greasing

150g dates

75g walnuts

1 tablespoon clear honey or golden
   syrup

finely grated zest of 1 lemon

100g fine oatmeal

25g self-raising flour

3 tablespoons Splenda granulated
   sweetener

1 teaspoon vanilla extract

1 egg, beaten

extra oatmeal, for dusting

These little cookies are golden on the outside, yet slightly soft in the centre – perfect for a reasonably healthy snack to serve with tea or coffee. They'd also work well with other firm-textured dried fruit such as figs, or with any other nuts.

Preheat the oven to 220°C/425°F/gas mark 7. Grease a large baking sheet. Whizz the dates in a food processor until chopped into small pieces. Add the walnuts and blend again until chopped.

Melt the butter in a medium saucepan with the honey or syrup and lemon zest. Tip in the dates and walnuts, oatmeal, flour, sweetener and vanilla and stir until mixed. Add the egg and beat to a thick paste.

Take spoonfuls of the mixture and shape into balls. Flatten onto the baking sheet, spacing them slightly apart. Sprinkle with extra oatmeal and bake for 10 minutes or until golden brown around the edges. Transfer to a wire rack to cool.

Per serving: 153kcal; 3g protein; 9g fat; 3.4g saturated fat; 16g carbohydrates; 8.8g sugar; 1.2g fibre; 0.03g sodium

apricot and ginger teabread

SERVES 12

200g ready-to-eat dried apricots,
   chopped
2 pieces stem ginger in syrup, finely
   chopped
50g raisins
300ml orange juice
½ teaspoon vegetable or
   sunflower oil
225g self-raising flour
8 tablespoons Splenda granulated
   sweetener
2 eggs, beaten

Melinda says: I love apricots and I love ginger and the combination in this recipe is out of this world. The perfect accompaniment to a cup of tea after a long day's work.

Mix together the apricots, stem ginger, raisins and orange juice and leave to soak for 30 minutes. Grease and line the base of a 900g loaf tin using the oil and greaseproof paper.

Preheat the oven to 180°C/350°F/gas mark 4. Sift the flour into a large bowl and stir in the sweetener.

Beat the eggs into the apricot mixture. Make a well in the middle of the flour and add the apricot mixture gradually, beating to make a batter. Pour into the prepared tin and bake for 45 minutes until golden.

To make sure the teabread is cooked, insert a skewer into the centre. If it comes out clean, the bread is done. If not, bake for a little longer. Leave to cool in the tin for 10 minutes, then place on a wire rack to cool completely. Serve in slices.

The teabread is suitable for freezing. It can be stored in an airtight container in the fridge for three to four days.

Per serving: 135kcal; 4g protein; 1g fat; 0.4g saturated fat; 29g carbohydrates; 14.6g sugar; 2g fibre; 0.09g sodium

coconut, apricot and passionfruit slices

SERVES 12

175g unsalted butter, softened, plus
  extra for greasing

50g creamed coconut

8 tablespoons Splenda granulated
  sweetener

3 eggs, beaten

75g self-raising flour

1 teaspoon baking powder

2 teaspoons vanilla extract

100g desiccated coconut

100g ready-to-eat dried apricots,
  chopped

for the glaze:

50g ready-to-eat dried apricots,
  chopped

75ml freshly squeezed orange juice

2 passionfruit

1 teaspoon Splenda granulated
  sweetener

coconut shavings, lightly toasted, to
  decorate

This simple tray bake is a tempting combination of coconut and naturally sweet, fruity flavours. It's best served on the day you make it as both the cake and topping will dry out overnight. To make the coconut shavings, pare strips of flesh from a fresh coconut and toast them lightly under a hot grill.

Preheat the oven to 180°C/350°F/gas mark 4. Grease and line a 27x18cm shallow, rectangular baking tin with greaseproof paper.

Put the butter, creamed coconut and sweetener in a bowl and beat with a hand-held electric whisk until pale and creamy. (If the creamed coconut is very firm, you can soften it first in the microwave.) Gradually beat in the eggs, one at a time, beating well after each addition. Sift the flour and baking powder into the bowl and stir in along with the vanilla, coconut and chopped apricots.

Turn into the tin and level the surface. Bake for 25 minutes until just firm to the touch.

Meanwhile, make the glaze. Heat the apricots and orange juice in a small saucepan for 5 minutes. Tip into a food processor and add the pulp from the passionfruit and the sweetener. Blend until smooth.

Transfer the cake to a cooling rack and leave to cool. Using a spoon, drizzle the apricot and passionfruit glaze over the cake and scatter generously with coconut shavings. Serve cut into fingers.

Per serving: 249kcal; 4g protein; 20g fat; 14g saturated fat; 14g carbohydrates; 8.7g sugar; 2.4g fibre; 0.1g sodium

white chocolate and orange scones

MAKES 12

40g unsalted butter, cut into small
  pieces, plus extra for greasing
225g self-raising flour
1 teaspoon baking powder
finely grated zest of 1 small orange
4 teaspoons Splenda granulated
  sweetener
100g white chocolate, chopped into
  very small pieces
150ml semi-skimmed milk, plus 1
  tablespoon to glaze

These sweet, orangey scones are best served freshly baked, but can also be frozen and warmed through when you serve them. For a summer version, try leaving out the white chocolate and serving them with strawberry jam and clotted cream instead.

Preheat the oven to 220°C/425°F/gas mark 7. Grease a baking sheet.

Put the flour and baking powder into a food processor. Add the butter and whizz until the mixture resembles fine breadcrumbs.

Add the orange zest and 3 teaspoons of the sweetener and blend briefly to combine. Add the chocolate and milk and blend again to make a soft dough.

Tip out onto a lightly floured work surface and roll out to a 2cm thickness. Cut out rounds using a 5cm round cutter and transfer to the baking sheet.

Mix the remaining sweetener with the tablespoon of milk and use to glaze the tops of the scones. Bake for about 10 minutes or until well risen and golden. Transfer to a wire rack to cool.

Per serving: 138kcal; 3g protein; 6g fat; 3.4g saturated fat; 20g carbohydrates; 5.9g sugar; 0.6g fibre; 0.13g sodium

pear crisp

SERVES 8

175g unsalted butter, cut into cubes,
  plus extra for greasing
6 Conference pears, peeled, cored and
  cubed
juice of 2 oranges
8 tablespoons Splenda granulated
  sweetener
pinch of ground nutmeg
pinch of ground cinnamon
25g powdered milk
50g ground almonds
25g rolled oats
175g unsalted butter, cut into cubes,
  plus extra for greasing
50g desiccated coconut
175g plain flour
½ teaspoon salt
50g flaked almonds, toasted

This is the American equivalent of a crumble. The oats, almonds, coconut and spices make a lovely, crunchy topping.

Preheat the oven to 200°C/400°F/gas mark 6. Grease the bottom of a deep baking dish with butter.

Combine the pears with the orange juice, 2 tablespoons of the sweetener, the nutmeg and cinnamon, and place in the baking dish.

In a food processor, pulse together the powdered milk, ground almonds and rolled oats. Add the butter, coconut, flour, remaining sweetener and salt and continue to pulse until the mixture is crumbly. Fold in the toasted almonds.

Pop the mixture on top of the pears and bake in the oven for about 40 minutes, or until the top is golden. This dish is delicious served hot with thick double or clotted cream.

Per serving: 618kcal; 7g protein; 51g fat; 28.3g saturated fat; 36g carbohydrates; 16.5g sugar; 5g fibre; 0.15g sodium

chocolate lovers

chocolate mousse cake

SERVES 6

50g unsalted butter, plus extra for
  greasing
100g ready-to-eat pitted prunes,
  chopped
2 tablespoons Cointreau, Grand Marnier
  or other orange liqueur
250g good-quality dark chocolate,
  broken into pieces
6 eggs, separated
4 tablespoons Splenda granulated
  sweetener
cocoa powder, for dusting
200g raspberries

This densely chocolatey pudding is dotted with liqueur-steeped prunes which means there's no need to add lots of sugar. For the best result, cook until barely set in the centre and serve warm with pouring cream so the flavours mingle together.

Preheat the oven to 160°C/325°F/gas mark 3. Grease and line the base of a 20cm loose base cake tin or springform tin with greaseproof paper.

Put the prunes and liqueur in a small saucepan with 1 tablespoon water and heat gently until bubbling around the edges. Remove from the heat.

Put the chocolate and butter in a heatproof bowl over a saucepan of barely simmering water and stir until melted. Alternatively, melt in the microwave for 1½ minutes at maximum power.

Whisk the egg yolks in a bowl with the sweetener for 2–3 minutes until slightly thickened. Whisk the egg whites in a grease-free bowl until they hold their shape. Stir the melted chocolate mixture, the prunes and any unabsorbed liqueur into the yolk mixture. Immediately fold in a third of the whisked egg whites using a large metal spoon, then fold in the remainder.

Scoop into the tin, spreading the mixture gently to the edges. Bake for 18–20 minutes or until the cake has risen and forms a soft crust. The cake should still feel wobbly underneath when the tin is shaken.

Leave in the tin for 10 minutes, then carefully transfer to a serving plate. Dust with the cocoa powder and scatter with the raspberries.

Per serving: 471kcal; 11g protein; 33g fat; 16.2g saturated fat; 32g carbohydrates; 23.4g sugar; 4.7g fibre; 0.07g sodium

chocolate orange cheesecake

SERVES 8

for the biscuit base:
75g butter
150g digestive biscuits, crushed

for the filling:
25g butter
110g plain chocolate, broken into pieces
1 tablespoon cocoa powder
2 tablespoons Cointreau or brandy
1 tablespoon powdered gelatine
200g cream cheese
2 teaspoons finely grated orange zest
4 tablespoons Splenda granulated
   sweetener
2 eggs, separated

This lovely cheesecake is perfect for a special occasion. Make it the day before, then decorate shortly before serving.

For the biscuit base, melt the butter in a saucepan over a low heat. Stir in the crushed biscuits. Tip into a 20cm loose-bottomed flan tin or dish and press into an even layer. Chill in the refrigerator until firm.

For the filling, put the butter, chocolate pieces, cocoa and Cointreau or brandy into a heatproof bowl. Sit the bowl over a saucepan of simmering water and allow to melt, stirring occasionally to blend. Cool slightly.

Put 75ml of just-boiled water into a bowl or jug. Sprinkle in the powdered gelatine, stirring to disperse it. Leave it to dissolve for about 3 minutes, stirring from time to time, until the liquid is perfectly clear.

Beat the cream cheese in a large mixing bowl to soften it, then mix in the orange zest, sweetener and egg yolks. Stir in the cooled chocolate mixture.

Whisk the egg whites in a grease-free bowl until stiff. Use a large metal spoon to fold them into the chocolate mixture, then fold in the gelatine liquid. Pour over the biscuit base and chill until firm – this will take 2–3 hours.

Decorate the cheesecake to your liking. I've used whipped cream, chocolate curls and shreds of orange zest.

Per serving: 497kcal; 6g protein; 40g fat; 23g saturated fat; 28g carbohydrates; 17.1g sugar; 1g fibre; 0.29g sodium

pain au chocolat

MAKES 16

400g strong white bread flour

1 teaspoon salt

1 tablespoon Splenda granulated
   sweetener

1 x 7g sachet dried yeast

165g unsalted butter, softened

1 egg, beaten

flour, for dusting

2 egg yolks, beaten

175g good-quality dark chocolate,
   broken into pieces

Nothing beats a homemade pain au chocolat!

Mix the flour, salt, sweetener and yeast in a bowl. Melt 15g of the butter and add to the bowl with the beaten egg and 200ml of warm water. Mix to a soft dough with a round-bladed knife. Turn out onto a floured surface and knead for 10 minutes until smooth and elastic.

Put the dough in a lightly oiled bowl and cover with clingfilm. Leave to rise in a warm place until doubled in size, about 1 hour. Roll the remaining butter between two sheets of greaseproof paper to a rectangle that measures roughly 30x7.5cm. Chill until firm.

Punch the dough to deflate it and tip onto a lightly floured surface. Roll out to a rectangle that's slightly larger than the rectangle of butter, with a short end facing you. Peel the paper away from the butter and place it over the dough. Fold the bottom third of the dough up and the top third down to create a thick block of dough with three layers of butter inside. Give the dough a quarter turn and repeat the rolling and folding twice more, giving the dough a quarter turn each time. Chill for 15 minutes then roll, fold and turn twice more. Chill again for 30 minutes.

Lightly grease two baking sheets. Mix the egg yolks with 1 teaspoon water. Roll out the dough on a lightly floured surface to a 35cm square. (If the dough shrinks as you roll it, cover it and leave to rest for 10 minutes.) Cut into 16 squares.

Press the chocolate pieces into the centre of each square. Brush the edges of each square with egg yolk. Roll up into sausage shapes and space apart on the baking sheet. Cover with greased clingfilm and leave to rise for 30–40 minutes until doubled in size. Preheat the oven to 200°C/400°F/gas mark 6.

Brush the dough generously with egg yolk to glaze and bake for about 20 minutes until deep golden. Transfer to a wire rack to cool.

Per serving: 237kcal; 5g protein; 14g fat; 8g saturated fat; 24g carbohydrates; 3.5g sugar; 1.4g fibre; 0.13g sodium

sachertorte

SERVES 12

175g unsalted butter, softened, plus
  extra for greasing
250g good-quality dark chocolate,
  broken into pieces
6 tablespoons brandy or almond liqueur
10 tablespoons Splenda granulated
  sweetener
5 eggs, separated
125g self-raising flour
100g ground almonds

for the glaze:
4 tablespoons apricot jam
  (see recipe page 80)
1 tablespoon brandy or almond liqueur
150ml double cream
100g good-quality dark chocolate,
  chopped
25g milk chocolate, chopped

A traditional Austrian Sachertorte is densely rich and smothered in a dark, glossy chocolate syrup with 'Sacher' piped on top. This simplified version is equally rich and delicious but uses a chocolate cream glaze. Store the cake in a cool place rather than the fridge for the best result.

Preheat the oven to 160°C/325°F/gas mark 3. Grease and line the base and sides of a 20cm round cake tin with greaseproof paper. Grease the paper. Put the dark chocolate and liqueur into a heatproof bowl and place it over a saucepan of barely simmering water. Leave until melted, stirring frequently. Alternatively, melt in the microwave for 1½ minutes at maximum power.

Beat the butter and sweetener with a hand-held electric whisk until pale and creamy. Stir in the melted chocolate, then the egg yolks, flour and almonds.

Whisk the egg whites in a grease-free bowl until stiff. Fold a quarter of the egg whites into the chocolate mixture with a large metal spoon, then fold in the rest.

Turn into the tin and level the surface. Bake for 30–35 minutes or until a skewer, inserted into the centre, comes out clean. Leave in the tin for 10 minutes then transfer to a wire rack to cool completely.

To make the glaze, press the apricot jam through a sieve into a small bowl and stir in the liqueur. Pour onto and brush all over the cake. Put the cream and dark chocolate in a heatproof bowl and rest it over a saucepan of barely simmering water. Stir until melted. Melt the milk chocolate in the same way, or microwave on medium power for 1 minute.

Pour the dark chocolate mixture over the top of the cake and spread to the edges and down the sides with a palette knife. Using a teaspoon, scribble lines of milk chocolate over the top of the cake to decorate.

Per serving: 505kcal; 8g protein; 38g fat; 18.8g saturated fat; 29g carbohydrates; 16.2g sugar; 2.6g fibre; 0.08g sodium

chocolate brownies

MAKES 15

250g plain chocolate, chopped
175g unsalted butter
3 eggs
25g Splenda granulated sweetener
60g self-raising flour
1 teaspoon baking powder
100g walnuts, roughly chopped

Melinda says: Everyone loves chocolate brownies! I make these for the family all the time and treat my kids to them after school – they don't stay on the plate for long!

Preheat the oven to 190°C/375°F/gas mark 5. Grease and line a shallow 27x18cm baking tin with greaseproof paper.

Put the chocolate and butter in a heatproof bowl and rest it over a saucepan of gently simmering water. Leave until melted, stirring frequently. Alternatively melt in the microwave for 2 minutes at maximum power.

Whisk the eggs in a bowl, gradually whisking in the sweetener until combined. Whisk in the melted chocolate mixture. Sift the flour and baking powder into the bowl. Add the walnuts and stir the ingredients together until just combined.

Turn into the tin and spread the mixture into the corners. Bake for about 15 minutes or until the surface is set but the mixture feels very soft underneath. Leave to cool in the tin. Cut into squares and store in an airtight tin.

Per serving: 252kcal; 3g protein; 20g fat; 9.5g saturated fat; 16g carbohydrates; 12.3g sugar; 0.8g fibre; 0.07g sodium

chocolate cherry sundaes

SERVES 4

250g fresh cherries

2 tablespoons Splenda granulated
  sweetener

1 teaspoon cornflour, blended with 1
  tablespoon cold water

100g low fat soft cheese

2 tablespoons semi-skimmed milk

½ teaspoon vanilla extract

for the chocolate sauce:

50g dark chocolate, broken into pieces

2 teaspoons cocoa powder

1 teaspoon cornflour, blended with 1
  tablespoon cold water

2 tablespoons golden syrup

If you've ever eaten Black Forest gâteau, you'll know how good the combination of cherries and chocolate is. Then try them together again in this fabulous dessert.

Reserve 4 cherries for decoration, then halve and stone the rest. Put them into a small saucepan with 150ml water and 1 tablespoon sweetener. Simmer for 3–4 minutes, until softened. Stir in the blended cornflour and cook, while stirring, until thickened. Remove from the heat and cool, stirring occasionally to prevent a skin from forming.

Meanwhile, beat together the low fat soft cheese, milk, vanilla extract and remaining sweetener until smooth.

Make the chocolate sauce by putting the chocolate, cocoa powder, blended cornflour and golden syrup into a small saucepan. Heat, stirring constantly, until smooth and blended. Cool for a few minutes, stirring to prevent a skin from forming.

Spoon the cherries, chocolate sauce and soft cheese mixture into layers in pretty serving glasses. Pop a fresh cherry on top of each one, then chill until ready to serve.

Per serving: 160kcal; 4g protein; 5g fat; 3g saturated fat; 25g carbohydrates; 21.9g sugar; 1g fibre; 0.13g sodium

chocolate ice cream

SERVES 6

5 egg yolks
3 tablespoons Splenda granulated
  sweetener
500ml milk
150g good-quality milk chocolate,
  broken into small pieces
250ml double cream

It is thought that as far back as 200BC, the Chinese ate some version of ice cream, and that the Roman Emperor Nero is said to have had a passion for it. The best ice cream for me is a homemade, custard-based chocolate ice cream – made with good quality chocolate.

Whisk the egg yolks with the sweetener in a bowl until light and frothy. In a small pan, heat the milk, bringing it to boiling point for just a couple of seconds. Remove from the heat and pour the hot milk into the egg yolk mixture, stirring all the time. Then pour the whole lot back into the saucepan and gently reheat, stirring constantly, until the custard is thickened. Don't allow the custard to boil or it will curdle!

Once thickened, drop in the chocolate pieces. Stir until the chocolate is melted and well combined with the custard. Remove from the heat and allow the mixture to cool. Chill in the freezer for a couple of hours until slushy.

Whip the double cream until you have soft peaks. Mix this into the chocolate and transfer to an ice-cream machine. Churn according to the instructions. Eat and enjoy!

Per serving: 440kcal; 8g protein; 38g fat; 19.9g saturated fat; 17g carbohydrates; 12.4g sugar; 1.5g fibre; 0.06g sodium

simple chocolate soufflé

SERVES 4

butter, for greasing

25g nuts, finely chopped

2 teaspoons cocoa powder

25g cornflour

225ml milk

120g dark chocolate (minimum 70% cocoa solids), broken into pieces

1 tablespoon instant coffee granules

5 tablespoons Splenda granulated sweetener, plus 1 teaspoon

3 egg yolks

5 egg whites

Don't be scared of the old soufflé. As long as you follow the rules and stick to the recipe, it'll work, I promise. Remember to have your guests ready and waiting at the table so you can bring the soufflé straight from the oven to the table. You can make the either in a large dish or in individual dishes.

Preheat the oven to 190°C/375°F/gas mark 5. Liberally butter a 1.5 litre soufflé dish and sprinkle the butter with the finely chopped nuts and cocoa powder.

Mix the cornflour with a little of the milk to a smooth paste.

Heat the remaining milk with the dark chocolate and coffee granules in a saucepan. Add the 5 tablespoons sweetener and stir until the chocolate has completely melted.

Pour in the cornflour paste and boil for 1 minute until thickened. Remove from the heat and stir in the egg yolks, one by one. Leave to cool a little while you whisk the egg whites in a grease-free bowl until stiff. Fold the egg whites and the remaining sweetener into the chocolate mixture.

Pour into the prepared soufflé dish and cook for 35 minutes. Serve immediately.

Per serving: 406kcal; 12g protein; 27g fat; 9.5g saturated fat; 30g carbohydrates; 17.8g sugar; 2.9g fibre; 0.13g sodium

cherry, apricot and chocolate chip flapjacks

MAKES 16

175g butter, plus extra for greasing

175g golden syrup

4 tablespoons Splenda granulated
 sweetener

300g porridge oats

pinch of salt

50g dried cherries, halved

75g ready-to-eat dried apricots, chopped

40g white chocolate chips

40g dark or milk chocolate chips

The dried cherries and chocolate chips give these flapjacks a delicious new twist!

Preheat the oven to 180°C/350°F/gas mark 4. Grease a 20cm square baking tin and line it with greaseproof paper – by leaving an overhang of paper, the flapjacks will be easier to remove later.

Melt the butter with the golden syrup in a large saucepan over a gentle heat. Bring to the boil and cook for 2 minutes, stirring constantly. Remove from the heat.

Mix together the sweetener, porridge oats, salt, cherries, apricots and chocolate chips. Add to the saucepan and stir together until thoroughly mixed. Tip into the prepared tin and level the surface with the back of a spoon.

Bake for 20–25 minutes until golden brown. Cool for 30 minutes, then remove from the tin and cut into 16 squares. Leave to cool completely on a wire rack. Keep in an airtight container, or wrap in greaseproof paper.

Per serving: 229kcal; 4g protein; 12g fat; 6.8g saturated fat; 29g carbohydrates; 16.2g sugar; 2.4g fibre; 0.15g sodium

cakes and muffins

carrot cake muffins

MAKES 10

300g wholemeal plain flour
2 teaspoons baking powder
1 teaspoon mixed spice
½ teaspoon salt
50g ground almonds
1 large egg, beaten
1 teaspoon vanilla extract
100ml vegetable oil
100ml semi-skimmed milk
12 tablespoons Splenda granulated
   sweetener
finely grated zest of 1 orange
350g carrots, peeled and finely grated
50g raisins

for the icing:
150g low fat soft cheese
1 tablespoon Splenda granulated
   sweetener

If you love carrot cake, then you'll adore these muffins...

Preheat the oven to 200°C/400°F/gas mark 6. Place ten paper muffin cases into a muffin tray, or use squares of greaseproof paper.

Sift the flour, baking powder, mixed spice and salt into a large mixing bowl. (Add any bran bits left in the sieve from the wholemeal flour back to the bowl.) Stir in the ground almonds.

Beat together the egg, vanilla extract, vegetable oil, milk, sweetener and most of the orange zest. Add the grated carrots and stir well.

Tip the wet ingredients and raisins into the bowl with dry ingredients. Stir until just combined. Avoid over-mixing and do not beat. Spoon the mixture into the paper muffin cases. Transfer to the oven and bake for 20–25 minutes until risen and golden. Cool on a wire rack.

To make the icing, mix together the soft cheese and sweetener until smooth. Top the muffins with the icing and sprinkle them with the reserved orange zest.

Per serving: 288kcal; 7g protein; 14g fat; 2.2g saturated fat; 35g carbohydrates; 11.4g sugar; 2.4g fibre; 0.31g sodium

fresh strawberry sponge cake

SERVES 8

40g unsalted butter, melted, plus extra
    for greasing
25g caster sugar
4 tablespoons Splenda granulated
    sweetener
5 eggs
100g plain flour

for the topping:
400g strawberries, hulled
1 tablespoon Splenda granulated
    sweetener
200ml double cream

This cake uses a Genoise sponge as a base – a light and airy whisked sponge – with the addition of melted butter that adds extra flavour and moisture, and makes it keep slightly longer. It's delicious served as it is here, in a single layer with whipped cream and fresh strawberries, or you can sandwich the cream and fruit between two layers.

Preheat the oven to 180°C/350°F/gas mark 4. Grease and base line two 20cm loose base sandwich tins.

Put the sugar, sweetener and eggs in a large heatproof bowl over a saucepan of barely simmering water and whisk with a hand-held electric whisk until the whisk leaves a trail when lifted from the bowl. Remove from the heat and whisk for a further 2 minutes.

Pour the melted butter around the edges of the mixture. Sift half the flour into the bowl and fold in with the butter, using a large metal spoon. Sift the remaining flour into the bowl and fold in. Divide between the tins and spread gently to the edges.

Bake for 18–20 minutes until pale golden around the edges and just firm to the touch. Loosen the edges and transfer to a wire rack to cool. Meanwhile, make a sauce by blitzing half the strawberries with the Splenda in a food processor. Pass through a sieve into a little bowl. Slice the remaining strawberries.

Whisk the double cream until it forms soft peaks. Spread over the cake, and top with the sliced strawberries and the sauce.

Per serving: 284kcal; 6g protein; 22g fat; 11.4g saturated fat; 17g carbohydrates; 7.8g sugar; 0.9g fibre; 0.05g sodium

ricotta cake

SERVES 12

vegetable oil, for greasing
250g unsalted butter, softened
100g caster sugar
4 tablespoons Splenda granulated
  sweetener
8 eggs, separated
finely grated zest of 2 oranges
finely grated zest of 3 lemons
200g mixed dried fruits
85g roasted hazelnuts, roughly chopped
250g ricotta cheese
85g plain flour

This cake is good for even the most wobbly of cooks. I've used whole cranberries, cherries and blueberries, and chopped apricots but you can mix and match what you have in the store cupboard or what appeals when out shopping. Equally you can use other nuts too.

Preheat the oven to 180°C/350°F/gas mark 4. Grease a 23x5cm springform cake tin sparingly with vegetable oil.

Cream the butter, sugar and sweetener together until pale and fluffy. Add the egg yolks one by one, beating well between each addition.

In a separate bowl, fold the citrus zest, dried fruits and nuts into the ricotta. Fold in the butter and egg mixture. Sift the flour into this mix and combine.

Beat the egg whites to soft peaks. Mix 1 tablespoon of the egg whites into the ricotta mix. Once this is amalgamated, fold in the remainder carefully, ensuring that you do not lose too much of the air.

Pour the mixture into the prepared cake tin and bake for 50 minutes. The rule about inserting the tip of a knife into the centre and coming out clean does not apply to this cake as it is very moist. The best way to tell if it is cooked is to shake the tin gently; if the cake wobbles very slightly, it needs just a little while longer to finish cooking.

Per serving: 397kcal; 8g protein; 28g fat; 13.8g saturated fat; 29g carbohydrates; 22.8g sugar; 1.5g fibre; 0.07g sodium

apple, apricot and sultana crumble cake

SERVES 8

10 tablespoons Splenda granulated
   sweetener
150g porridge oats
100g muesli
1 teaspoon mixed spice
150g butter, melted
1 egg, beaten
2 Cox's eating apples, peeled, cored
   and sliced
1 tablespoon lemon juice
100g ready-to-eat dried apricots,
   chopped
50g sultanas
natural yogurt, single cream or ice
   cream, to serve

You'll love this delicious cake – it's great for teatime or as a pudding.

Preheat the oven to 180°C/350°F/gas mark 4. Grease and line an 18cm round loose-base cake tin.

Mix together the sweetener, porridge oats, muesli and mixed spice. Stir in the melted butter, then mix in the beaten egg. In a separate bowl, mix together the apple slices, lemon juice, apricots and sultanas.

Tip about two thirds of the muesli mixture into the prepared cake tin. Press down lightly and arrange half the fruit mixture on top. Sprinkle with the remaining crumble mixture and level the surface. Top with the remaining fruit, pressing it down lightly again.

Bake for 35–40 minutes until firm and golden brown. Place the cake tin on a wire rack and leave to cool for 15–20 minutes. Carefully remove the cake from the tin and peel away the paper lining. Serve warm or cold with natural yogurt, cream or ice cream.

Per serving: 324kcal; 6g protein; 18g fat; 10.4g saturated fat; 36g carbohydrates; 17.3g sugar; 4.3g fibre; 0.18g sodium

bakewell tarts

SERVES 8

350g puff pastry, thawed if frozen

flour, for dusting

8 teaspoons raspberry or strawberry jam

75g butter, softened

6 tablespoons Splenda granulated
   sweetener

1 egg, beaten

100g ground almonds

Puff pastry gives a lovely lift to these melt-in-the-mouth almond tarts. They're lovely served with custard or single cream.

Preheat the oven to 200°C/400°F/gas mark 6.

Roll out the pastry on a lightly floured work surface. Use a 10cm fluted cutter to stamp out 8 rounds, then use them to line 8 Yorkshire pudding tins or individual tart tins. Prick the bases with a fork. Place 1 teaspoon of jam into each one, spreading it over the middle of the pastry. Stand the tins on a baking tray.

Beat together the butter, sweetener, beaten egg and ground almonds. Share this mixture between the tarts, spreading it out to cover the jam.

Bake for 20–25 minutes, until the pastry is risen and golden brown. Leave them to cool for a few minutes before serving.

Per serving: 336kcal; 6g protein; 26g fat; 9.7g saturated fat; 22g carbohydrates; 5.7g sugar; 0.9g fibre; 0.2g sodium

moist cherry cake

SERVES 8

250g unsalted butter, softened, plus
    extra for greasing
350g fresh cherries
8 tablespoons Splenda granulated
    sweetener
5 eggs, separated
1 teaspoon almond extract
150g ground almonds
100g self-raising flour

Melinda says: This recipe gives you the chance to make the most of fresh cherries during their season. I really like making this cake at the weekend with help from my daughter – and I always catch her licking the spoon...

Preheat the oven to 180°C/350°F/gas mark 4. Grease and line the base and sides of a 20cm loose-base cake tin or springform tin. Grease the paper. Halve and stone the cherries.

Using a hand-held electric whisk, whisk together the butter and all but 2 tablespoons of the sweetener until pale, creamy and very soft. Whisk in the egg yolks, almond extract, ground almonds, flour and 1 tablespoon warm water.

Whisk the egg whites in a thoroughly clean bowl until they form soft peaks, then whisk in the remaining sweetener. Using a large metal spoon, gently fold a quarter of the egg whites into the almond mixture. Gently fold in the remainder with half the cherries.

Turn the mixture into the tin and spread it out in an even layer. Scatter the remaining cherries on top. Bake for about 50 minutes until the cake is risen and firm to the touch. Test by piercing the centre of the cake with a skewer – it should come out fairly clean. Leave to cool in the tin then transfer to a serving plate. The cake can be stored for a couple of days without drying out.

Per serving: 460kcal; 9g protein; 40g fat; 18g saturated fat; 17g carbohydrates; 7.3g sugar; 2.1g fibre; 0.09g sodium

apple and cinnamon muffins

MAKES 16

vegetable oil or butter, for greasing

2 tart apples, peeled, cored and diced

4 tablespoons Splenda granulated
   sweetener

100g unsalted butter

1 teaspoon lemon juice

100g plain flour

pinch of salt

3 teaspoons baking powder

3 teaspoons bicarbonate of soda

1 teaspoon ground cinnamon

2 eggs, lightly beaten

150ml milk

150ml golden syrup

**The combination of apples and cinnamon is more unusual than that
of plums and cinnamon, yet here the cinnamon makes the body of the
muffins extra rich and interesting.**

Preheat the oven to 180°C/350°F/gas mark 4. Grease a muffin tray with
vegetable oil or butter.

In a small saucepan, cook the apples together with 4 tablespoons of the
sweetener, 25g of the butter and the lemon juice until the apples are soft but not
mushy and the liquid has almost evaporated. Set aside to cool.

Sift the flour, salt, baking powder, bicarbonate of soda and cinnamon into a
bowl. Stir in the remaining sweetener.

Melt the remaining butter, then combine with the eggs, milk and golden syrup.
Gently stir in the apples.

Pour the wet mix over the flour mix and stir just enough to bind them. The batter
should not be smooth. Spoon into the prepared muffin tins so each hole is about
two-thirds full. Bake for about 20 minutes or until a skewer pushed into the
centre comes out clean. Cool on a wire rack.

Per serving: 141kcal; 2g protein; 6g fat; 3.5g saturated fat; 21g carbohydrates;
15.5g sugar; 0.4g fibre; 0.44g sodium

blueberry muffins

MAKES 12

4 tablespoons vegetable oil, plus extra
   for greasing
200g plain flour
2 teaspoons baking powder
3 tablespoons Splenda granulated
   sweetener
175ml milk or buttermilk
1 egg
200g blueberries, halved

You could use chocolate chips in place of the blueberries if you like.

Preheat the oven to 180°C/350°F/gas mark 4. Thoroughly grease a 12-hole muffin tray with vegetable oil. This is best done in advance so that the batter doesn't have to wait before being poured into the tray.

Sift the flour and baking powder into a large mixing bowl, and gently stir in the sweetener.

In a separate bowl, mix the milk, egg and the 4 tablespoons of oil together. Make a well in the centre of the flour and slowly fold in the liquid. When all the liquid is added, beat well, and add the blueberries.

Spoon the mixture into the prepared muffin tray so each hole is about two-thirds full. Bake in the oven for 20–25 minutes. You can test whether the muffins are cooked by pressing lightly on one; if the top springs back, they are ready.

Cool the muffins on a wire rack. You can eat them on their own, but I think they are best when served slightly warm, split, and spread with butter and jam.

Per serving: 129kcal; 3g protein; 5g fat; 0.8g saturated fat; 19g carbohydrates; 6.1g sugar; 0.8g fibre; 0.11g sodium

raspberry and banana muffins

MAKES 8

200g plain flour
2 teaspoons baking powder
8 tablespoons Splenda granulated
  sweetener
100g frozen raspberries, briefly
  thawed
1 egg
1 teaspoon vanilla extract
50g butter, melted
100ml semi-skimmed milk
1 ripe banana, mashed

I've used frozen raspberries in this recipe as they tend to have a more intense flavour than fresh ones.

Preheat the oven to 200°C/400°F/gas mark 6. Place 8 paper muffin cases into a muffin tray, or use squares of greaseproof paper.

Sift the flour and baking powder into a large mixing bowl. Stir in the sweetener and raspberries.

Beat together the egg, vanilla extract, melted butter and milk. Stir into the dry ingredients with the mashed banana until just combined. Avoid overmixing and do not beat. The mixture will be quite lumpy, but there should not be any traces of dry flour. Spoon into the paper cases.

Bake for 20–25 minutes until risen and golden. Cool on a wire rack.

Per serving: 171kcal; 4g protein; 6g fat; 3.6g saturated fat; 26g carbohydrates; 6g sugar; 1.2g fibre; 0.2g sodium

porter cake

SERVES 8

175g unsalted butter, cut into cubes,
  plus extra for greasing
500g mixed dried fruit
finely grated zest of 1 lemon
8 tablespoons Splenda granulated
  sweetener
1 tablespoon black treacle
200ml porter or stout
1 teaspoon bicarbonate of soda
3 eggs, beaten
250g plain flour
1 tablespoon mixed spice

**Porter is a dark, richly flavoured beer that, like stout and Guinness, adds
a great flavour to rich fruit cakes. This simple fruit cake is so easy to
make and keeps very well for up to a week, if it lasts that long!**

Preheat the oven to 150°C/300°F/gas mark 2. Grease the base and sides of an
18cm round cake tin and line with greaseproof paper. Grease the paper too.

Put the butter, dried fruit, lemon zest, sweetener, treacle and porter or stout
in a large saucepan. Bring to the boil and stir frequently until the butter has
dissolved. Reduce the heat and simmer gently for 10 minutes until the juices are
thickened and syrupy. Leave to cool for 10 minutes.

Stir in the bicarbonate of soda so the mixture becomes foamy, then stir in the
beaten eggs. Sift in the flour and spice and mix until combined. Spoon into the
tin and level the surface.

Bake for about 1 hour or until a skewer, inserted into the centre, comes out
clean. Leave to cool in the tin. Store in an airtight container.

Per serving: 489kcal; 7g protein; 21g fat; 12.1g saturated fat; 71g carbohydrates;
46.5g sugar; 2.5g fibre; 0.24g sodium

angel cake

SERVES 8

2 teaspoons vegetable oil

75g plain flour, plus extra for dusting

50g caster sugar

10 tablespoons Splenda granulated
sweetener

8 egg whites

1 teaspoon cream of tartar

50g dried skimmed milk powder

1 teaspoon vanilla extract

pulp of 2 passionfruit

a handful of raspberries

for the frosting:

250g mascarpone cheese

300ml double cream

2 tablespoons Limoncello or other citrus
liqueur

2 tablespoons lemon juice

1 teaspoon Splenda granulated
sweetener

This sweet, vanilla-scented sponge can be made using a decorative kugelhopf tin or a plain ring tin – as long as there's a hole in the centre to allow for quick, even cooking. Angel cake can be served just as it is, but for this recipe I've done something a little more special – I've smothered it in a liqueur and mascarpone frosting which completes its whiter than white appeal.

Preheat the oven to 160°C/325°F/gas mark 3. Brush a 1.5 litre kugelhopf or ring tin with the oil and coat with flour, tapping out the excess. Mix together the caster sugar and sweetener.

Whisk the egg whites in a thoroughly clean bowl until foamy. Add the cream of tartar and whisk again until stiff. Gradually whisk in the caster sugar and sweetener, a spoonful at a time. Stir in the milk powder and vanilla extract. Sift a thin layer of flour over the whisked mixture and fold in using a large metal spoon. Continue to sift and fold in the rest of the flour.

Turn the mixture into the tin and level the surface. Bake for 20–25 minutes until firm to the touch. Loosen the edges of the mould with a knife and invert onto a wire rack. Leave to cool with the tin still in position. (If the cake has risen well above the top of the tin, cut a little off but bear in mind that the cake will shrink back as it cools.) Once cool, transfer to a plate.

To make the frosting, beat the mascarpone in a bowl until softened. Add the cream, liqueur, lemon juice and sweetener and whisk until smooth. Using a palette knife, spread the cream mixture over the cake, swirling it decoratively with the tip of the knife. Scatter the fruits over the top of the cake to finish.

Per serving: 455kcal; 8g protein; 36g fat; 20.5g saturated fat; 25g carbohydrates; 16.9g sugar; 0.9g fibre; 0.35g sodium

fig streusel

SERVES 8

200ml red wine

2 teaspoons Splenda granulated
  sweetener

25g fresh ginger, peeled and grated

8 fresh figs, quartered

200g red grapes, halved

1½ teaspoons cornflour

for the streusel:

200g plain flour

1 teaspoon ground mixed spice

175g lightly salted butter, cut into small
  cubes

8 tablespoons Splenda granulated
  sweetener

75g ground almonds

1 egg

2 tablespoons flaked almonds, lightly
  toasted

Streusels are great for serving with a cup of coffee or, when freshly baked, as a dessert with dollops of whipped cream or crème fraîche. The red wine and ginger give the cake a warm, wintry flavour.

Preheat the oven to 180°C/350°F/gas mark 4. Grease a 23cm loose-base cake tin or springform tin.

Put the wine in a saucepan with the sweetener and ginger and bring slowly to the boil. Reduce the heat to a gentle simmer and add the figs and grapes. Turn the fruits gently in the syrup for 1 minute, then remove with a slotted spoon and place into a bowl.

Blend the cornflour with 1 tablespoon water and add to the pan. Bring to the boil, stirring until thickened. Pour over the fruits and stir gently to mix. Leave to cool while you make the streusel.

Put the flour and mixed spice into a food processor with the butter. Blend until the mixture resembles fine breadcrumbs. Add the sweetener and ground almonds and blend again until the mixture forms a coarse crumble. Weigh out 100g of the crumble mixture and set aside. Add the egg to the remaining mixture and blend to a paste.

Tip the paste into the tin and press down over the base and slightly up the sides of the tin to make a case. Bake for 15 minutes.

Scatter the fig mixture and juices over the case, piling them up slightly in the centre. Sprinkle the crumble mixture on top and scatter with the almonds. Bake for 30 minutes until pale golden. Leave to cool slightly in the tin, then serve warm or cold.

Per serving: 396kcal; 7g protein; 26g fat; 12.1g saturated fat; 34g carbohydrates; 13.7g sugar; 2.6g fibre; 0.15g sodium

jams, spreads and sauces

lemon curd

MAKES ABOUT 375G

zest and juice of 4 large unwaxed
 lemons
2 organic eggs, plus 2 egg yolks
150g unsalted butter, cut into small
 cubes
5 tablespoons Splenda granulated
 sweetener

**A fresh, zesty lemon curd is perfect for spreading over warm toast or
as a filling for a sponge cake. For a good, rich colour, make sure you
use organic eggs.**

Place all the ingredients in a large, heatproof bowl and place it over a saucepan
of gently simmering water. (Make sure the base of the bowl is not touching the
water or the mixture will overheat.)

Cook the mixture gently, stirring frequently with a wooden spoon until the butter
and sweetener have dissolved. Continue to cook, stirring constantly, until the
curd is thickened enough to thinly coat the back of the wooden spoon. This will
take about 15 minutes.

Strain through a sieve into sterilised jars (see below). Cover with discs of
greaseproof paper and lids and leave to cool. Store in the fridge – the curd will
keep for up to three weeks.

Per 25g serving: 96kcal; 1g protein; 10g fat; 5.6g saturated fat; 1g carbohydrates;
0.8g sugar; 0g fibre; 0.01g sodium

how to sterilise jars

To sterilise jars, wash the jars thoroughly in warm, soapy water, discarding
any old labels. Preheat the oven to 150°C/300°F/gas mark 2. Put the jars on
a baking sheet lined with kitchen paper and heat in the oven for 15 minutes.
Alternatively, run the upturned jars through a hot dishwasher cycle.

cranberry sauce

SERVES 6

4 tablespoons Splenda granulated
  sweetener
750g fresh or frozen cranberries
pinch of ground cinnamon
pinch of grated nutmeg
raisins, currants or orange peel
  (optional)

Fresh cranberries are a deep orangey red and can be found in our supermarkets in late autumn. They are also often dried to preserve them throughout the year. Cranberry sauce is an essential accompaniment to turkey at any American Thanksgiving dinner.

Put the sweetener and 250ml of water into a heavy-based saucepan and heat up gently to dissolve the sweetener. Add the cranberries, bring to the boil, and cook for 10 minutes until the berries burst.

Stir in the spices and, if using, any of the optional ingredients. Remove from the heat and leave to cool completely, then chill in the fridge.

Per serving: 25kcal; 1g protein; 0g fat; 0g saturated fat; 5g carbohydrates; 5.2g sugar; 3.8g fibre; 0g sodium

homemade chocolate-nut spread

MAKES ABOUT 450G

250g whole hazelnuts

3 tablespoons Splenda granulated
   sweetener

4 tablespoons (unsweetened) cocoa
   powder

½ teaspoon vanilla extract

4 tablespoons vegetable oil

When you really need a chocolate fix and there isn't a jar of Nutella to hand, this simple spread will do the trick. It's fun to make for the kids too. It can be stored in an airtight jar for up to one month.

Preheat the oven to 180°C/350°F/gas mark 4.

Spread the hazelnuts on a tray and toast them in the oven until the skins are blackened, turning them once – this will take around 15 minutes. Remove from the oven and leave to cool until you can handle them. Remove the bitter skins by putting the nuts into a paper bag and rubbing until most of the skins have come off. It doesn't matter if there are still specs of blackened skin on the nuts as long as you get rid of the vast majority.

Put the hazelnuts into a liquidiser and blitz – the nuts get crushed first, then become a fine powder and finally form a ball around the blade, making hazelnut butter. This will take about 5 minutes.

Add the sweetener, cocoa powder and vanilla essence and, with the liquidiser on a low speed, drizzle in enough oil to make the right consistency of chocolate spread.

Spoon the mixture into an airtight glass jar and store in the fridge. Stir the chocolate spread before using as it will solidify a little when chilled.

Per 25g serving: 121kcal; 2g protein; 12g fat; 1.1g saturated fat; 2g carbohydrates; 1g sugar; 1.1g fibre; 0g sodium

apricot jam

MAKES ABOUT 600G

1½ teaspoons gelatine powder

500g fresh apricots, stoned and roughly
  chopped

200ml apple juice

1 tablespoon lemon juice

8 tablespoons Splenda granulated
  sweetener

This delicious, tangy fruit spread technically isn't a jam – without sugar used in the method, it doesn't have the same preservative qualities a 'real' jam would have. It's therefore best made in small quantities and it keeps in the fridge for up to three weeks.

Put 2 tablespoons water into a bowl and stir in the gelatine. Leave to soak whilst you cook the apricots.

Put the apricots into a saucepan and pour in the apple and lemon juice. Bring to the boil, turn down the heat and simmer gently, uncovered, for about 10 minutes or until the apricots are soft. Skim off any foam that collects on the surface using a slotted spoon.

Remove the pan from the heat and stir in the sweetener. Add the gelatine and stir again until dissolved. Ladle into sterilised jars (see page 76) and cover with discs of greaseproof paper and lids whilst still hot.

Per 25g serving: 12kcal; 0g protein; 0g fat; 0g saturated fat; 3g carbohydrates; 2.7g sugar; 0.3g fibre; 0g sodium

mango and passionfruit sauce

SERVES 4

1 ripe mango, peeled and stoned

2 passionfruit, halved

2 tablespoons Splenda granulated
  sweetener

Cut the mango into chunks and scoop the flesh out of the passionfruit. Place the fruits into a food processor with the sweetener and whizz until you have a smooth purée. Scoop the purée into a sieve and push through into a nice bowl or jug.

The sauce can be stirred into yogurt, poured over a scoop of good ice cream or served with a fruit-filled pancake.

Per serving: 44kcal; 1g protein; 0g fat; 0g saturated fat; 11g carbohydrates; 10.5g sugar; 2g fibre; 0g sodium

blood orange curd

MAKES ABOUT 375ML

125ml blood orange juice

1 tablespoon finely grated blood orange
  zest

125g unsalted butter

1½ tablespoons Splenda granulated
  sweetener

3 eggs plus 1 egg yolk

Blood oranges are wonderful alternative to lemon in this recipe.

Put the orange juice, orange zest, butter and sweetener into a small pan and place on a gentle heat. Stir until the butter is melted and everything is mixed together thoroughly.

Remove the pan from the heat and slowly whisk in the eggs, one at a time, until the mixture thickens – this will take a few minutes. Finally, whisk in the egg yolk.

Cool the mixture and put into sterilised, airtight jars (see page 76). It will keep in the fridge for a couple of weeks. This curd is great on toast, as a filling for a tart or to make a Victoria sponge with a twist.

Per 25g serving: 84kcal; 2g protein; 8g fat; 4.7g saturated fat; 1g carbohydrates; 0.8g sugar; 0g fibre; 0.02g sodium

blackberry pickle

MAKES ABOUT 1.5KG

900g blackberries
2–3 tablespoons Splenda granulated
  sweetener
75ml apple juice
2 teaspoons allspice
2 tablespoons ground ginger
500ml white vinegar

We've been making pickles for years. This blackberry pickle is a nice combo with a strong, mature Cheddar cheese or with cold meats.

In a bowl, toss the blackberries gently in the sweetener, apple juice and the two spices and leave to rest overnight to allow the flavours to mingle.

Bring the vinegar to the boil, add the berries, reduce the heat and cook gently for 20 minutes. Allow to cool and spoon into sterilised jars (see page 76). The pickle keeps in the fridge for one month.

Per 25g serving: 18kcal; 0g protein; 0g fat; 0g saturated fat; 4g carbohydrates; 4g sugar; 0.5g fibre; 0g sodium

blackberry chutney

MAKES ABOUT 1.8KG

1.4kg blackberries
450g apples, peeled, cored and chopped
225g onions, finely chopped
1 teaspoon ground ginger
1 teaspoon English mustard powder
¼ teaspoon grated nutmeg
¼ teaspoon ground mace
10 tablespoons Splenda granulated
  sweetener
150ml apple juice
600ml white vinegar
sea salt and crushed black pepper

Place all the ingredients into a large, heavy based saucepan with 1 teaspoon salt and 1 teaspoon pepper. Bring to the boil, turn down the heat and simmer for about 1 hour until the desired consistency is reached, remembering that it will be a little thicker when cold.

Spoon into hot, sterilised jars (see page 76) and seal. Once cooled, store in the fridge. It will keep for up to one month.

Per 25g serving: 14kcal; 0g protein; 0g fat; 0g saturated fat; 3g carbohydrates; 3.2g sugar; 0.6g fibre; 0.02g sodium

apple, plum and date chutney

MAKES ABOUT 1.5KG

500g ready-to-eat dried apple slices,
  roughly chopped
1 large onion, chopped
375g plums, pitted and roughly chopped
50g dates, chopped
2 teaspoons salt
300ml white vinegar
10 tablespoons Splenda granulated
  sweetener
6 cloves
1 cinnamon stick

This fruity chutney is perfect for serving with a ploughman's lunch or with cold roast meats and cheese.

Put the apples into a large saucepan and cover with 1 litre just-boiled water. Bring to the boil, then reduce the heat and simmer gently for about an hour until the water has almost evaporated.

Add the remaining ingredients and cook gently, stirring often, until the chutney is thick and pulpy – this will take about 45 minutes. Make sure the chutney is about the right consistency at this point, as it will only thicken a little more as it cools.

Remove the cinnamon stick, then pot the chutney in warm, sterilised jars (see page 76) and seal whilst hot. Cool, then keep refrigerated and use within one month.

Per 25g serving: 22kcal; 0g protein; 0g fat; 0g saturated fat; 6g carbohydrates; 5.5g sugar; 0.8g fibre; 0.06g sodium

apple sauce

SERVES 4

1 large Bramley apple

2 Cox's apples

1 teaspoon Splenda granulated
sweetener

Melinda says: This is one of those sauces that is easy to prepare, yet so versatile. It makes a great accompaniment to a variety of sweet and savoury dishes.

Peel and core all apples and chop into dice. Toss in the sweetener, then put into a small saucepan with the water.

Place the pan on a low heat and gently bring to the boil. Cover and simmer on a very low heat until the apple is just soft.

Stir well and pour into a warmed serving bowl.

Per serving: 42kcal; 0g protein; 0g fat; 0g saturated fat; 10g carbohydrates; 10.4g sugar; 1.8g fibre; 0g sodium

occasional treats and seasonal goodies

wholemeal pancakes with simmered winter fruits

SERVES 4

for the pancakes:

110g wholemeal flour

pinch of salt

1 egg, beaten

300ml skimmed milk

1 teaspoon Splenda granulated
  sweetener

vegetable oil, for frying

for the fruit filling:

1 orange

250ml orange juice

25g ready-to-eat dried apricots, chopped

25g sultanas or raisins

pinch of mixed spice

1 apple, cored and sliced

2 plums, stoned and sliced

2 teaspoons cornflour

1 tablespoon Splenda granulated
  sweetener

Try these healthy pancakes, made with wholemeal flour – available from most supermarkets and health food stores. Alternatively, just make them with plain white flour.

Place the flour and salt into a large bowl with the egg, milk and sweetener. Beat together with a wire whisk to make a smooth pancake batter.

To make the filling, peel strips of zest from the orange using a potato peeler. Reserve 3 tablespoons of the orange juice, pour the rest into a saucepan and add the strips of zest, the apricots, sultanas or raisins, and mixed spice. Place on the heat and simmer gently for 10–15 minutes to plump up the fruit. Remove the orange zest. Meanwhile, cut the orange into segments, removing all the pith.

Drop the orange segments into the saucepan with the sliced apple and plums. Mix the cornflour with the reserved orange juice and add to the pan. Heat again gently, stirring until thickened and smooth. Stir in the sweetener, and keep warm over a low heat whilst making the pancakes.

Heat a large frying pan and add a few drops of vegetable oil. Pour in a thin stream of batter, tilting the pan so that it flows evenly across the surface. Cook over a medium heat until set, then flip the pancake over to cook the other side. Make four large pancakes in this way. Place on warm plates and serve immediately with the simmered fruit.

Per serving: 252kcal; 9g protein; 5g fat; 0.9g saturated fat; 45g carbohydrates; 25.2g sugar; 4.6g fibre; 0.21g sodium

hot cross buns

MAKES 10

375g strong white bread flour, plus extra
    for dusting
100g mixed dried fruit
finely grated zest of 1 lemon
2 teaspoons mixed spice
1 teaspoon ground cinnamon
1 x 7g sachet dried yeast
6 tablespoons Splenda granulated
    sweetener
1 egg, beaten
50g unsalted butter, melted, plus extra
    for greasing
200ml warm milk
oil, for greasing

for the crosses:
25g plain flour
2–3 tablespoons milk
1 egg, beaten

Although easy to make, you'll need to allow plenty of time to prove these spicy buns – they're made using a rich, fruity bread dough which takes longer to rise than a plainer dough. Once made, you can freeze any buns you won't be eating, warming them through in a moderate oven once thawed.

Put the bread flour, dried fruit, lemon zest, spices, yeast and 4 tablespoons of the sweetener in a mixing bowl and stir to combine. Add the egg, melted butter and milk and mix with a round-bladed knife to make a soft dough.

Turn out onto a floured surface and knead for 10 minutes until the dough is smooth and elastic. Place in a lightly oiled bowl, cover with clingfilm and leave to rise in a warm place for about 2 hours until the dough has doubled in size.

Lightly grease a large baking sheet. Push the air out of the dough and tip onto a lightly floured work surface. Divide into ten even-sized pieces and shape each into a ball. Place on the baking sheet, about 3cm apart, and flatten them slightly. Cover with greased clingfilm and leave to rise again for about 45 minutes until doubled in size.

Preheat the oven to 220°C/425°F/gas mark 7.

To make the crosses, mix the plain flour with the milk to make a soft paste. Spoon into a small polythene bag and squeeze the mixture into a corner. Brush the dough with beaten egg. Snip off the corner of the bag and pipe crosses onto the buns. Bake in the oven for 15–20 minutes until risen and golden.

Dissolve the remaining sweetener in 2 teaspoons hot water. Transfer the buns to a wire rack and brush with the glaze. Leave to cool.

Per serving: 227kcal; 6g protein; 6g fat; 3.2g saturated fat; 40g carbohydrates; 9.3g sugar; 1.5g fibre; 0.17g sodium

easter egg brownies

MAKES 12

100g good-quality dark chocolate,
  chopped
115g unsalted butter
3 eggs
5 tablespoons Splenda granulated
  sweetener
25g self-raising flour
2 tablespoons cocoa powder
1 teaspoon baking powder
125g milk chocolate, chopped

for the topping:
175g milk chocolate
36 chocolate mini eggs

In this recipe, rich chocolate brownies are baked as individual little cakes and finished with a chocolate mini egg topping. Like all chocolate brownie mixtures, they need very little cooking or they'll lose their moist texture.

Preheat the oven to 190°C/375°F/gas mark 5. Line a 12-section tartlet tray with paper cases.

Put the dark chocolate and butter in a heatproof bowl and place over a saucepan of barely simmering water. Stir frequently until the chocolate and butter are melted and mixed together. Alternatively, melt in the microwave and stir together.

Crack the eggs into a bowl and gradually whisk in the sweetener until combined, then whisk in the melted chocolate mixture. Sift the flour, cocoa powder and baking powder into the bowl. Add the chopped milk chocolate and stir the ingredients together until just combined.

Divide the mixture over the paper cases and bake in the oven for about 8 minutes or until just firm. Transfer to a wire rack to cool.

To decorate the brownies, shave 100g of the milk chocolate into small curls using a potato peeler. If the chocolate breaks off in brittle shards, pop it in the microwave for a few seconds and try again.

Melt the remaining milk chocolate and spread over the brownies. Top with the chocolate curls and the chocolate mini eggs. Delicious!

Per serving: 325kcal; 5g protein; 23g fat; 11.8g saturated fat; 27g carbohydrates; 23.4g sugar; 0.9g fibre; 0.11g sodium

star anise crème brûlée

SERVES 4

600ml double cream
3 star anise
6 large egg yolks
2 tablespoons Splenda granulated
   sweetener
caster sugar, for sprinkling

This dessert is a classic with a hint of the Orient. It needs to be refrigerated overnight, so a bit of organisation is required, but it's worth it for what is probably the greatest of British puds.

Put the cream and star anise into a saucepan and place on the heat. You want the cream to become quite hot, but you don't want to bring it to the boil. Remove the pan from the heat and leave to stand for 30 minutes to allow the flavours to permeate.

Beat the egg yolks and sweetener together. Strain the flavoured cream onto the egg mixture, whisk thoroughly and return to the heat. Cook over a medium heat and stir constantly with a wooden spoon. Don't use a whisk as you don't want to incorporate air into the custard. Cook until the custard coats the back of a spoon. (A good test is to cover the back of a spoon with the custard, then run your finger down the middle of the spoon; if the custard does not join up again, it is ready.) Keep a close eye on the pan, making sure the custard doesn't come to the boil, otherwise it will split and separate, producing rather expensive scrambled eggs.

Strain the custard into four largish ramekins and allow to cool, then place in the fridge and leave overnight.

A couple of hours before serving, preheat the grill and sprinkle each ramekin with a thin layer of caster sugar. Place the ramekins in an ice-filled tray and glaze the sugar under the grill until caramelised with delicious dark patches. Once the sugar has been caramelised, don't refrigerate the dishes again.

To serve, crack open the caramel and indulge.

Per serving: 891kcal; 8g protein; 91g fat; 48g saturated fat; 11g carbohydrates; 11.1g sugar; 0g fibre; 0.05g sodium

balsamic strawberries with mascarpone cream

SERVES 12

750g ripe strawberries, hulled
4 tablespoons aged balsamic vinegar
2 tablespoons Splenda granulated
  sweetener

for the mascarpone cream:
1 tablespoon Splenda granulated
  sweetener
3 egg yolks
4 teaspoons kirsch
225g mascarpone cheese
150ml double cream

The strawberries you find in the shops these days often need a little something to bring out their natural sweetness. In this recipe, the Splenda and balsamic vinegar help to do just that.

Mix the strawberries, balsamic vinegar and sweetener together and leave to marinate for around 30 minutes.

To make the mascarpone cream, beat together the sweetener and the egg yolks until the mixture has lightened to a pale yellow. Fold in the kirsch and the mascarpone. Whisk the double cream until it forms soft peaks and fold gently into the mascarpone mixture.

To serve the strawberries, scoop them into bowls and top with a generous dollop of the mascarpone cream.

Per serving: 191kcal; 2g protein; 17g fat; 9.7g saturated fat; 6g carbohydrates; 6.4g sugar; 0.7g fibre; 0.03g sodium

orange and cardamom ice cream

SERVES 3

250ml whole milk

finely grated zest of 2 oranges

6 tablespoons Splenda granulated
sweetener

110g vanilla sugar

1 tablespoon orange liqueur

1 egg

pinch of ground cardamom

600ml buttermilk

Good oranges and the richness of buttermilk make this a sublime ice cream, which is as refreshing after a big winter dinner as it is in the heat of summer.

Take a large saucepan and add all the ingredients except the buttermilk. Stir very thoroughly to make a lump-free custard and heat this over low heat, stirring frequently, until the mixture thickens.

Pour in the buttermilk and blend the mixture thoroughly until it is fully incorporated. Cook for a few minutes more but do not boil. Remove from the heat and leave to cool, covered.

Once cool, chill for a couple of hours in the fridge, then scoop into a ice-cream maker, 1–1.5 litres in size, and follow the manufacturer's instructions to churn and freeze.

Per serving: 326kcal; 12g protein; 6g fat; 3.2g saturated fat; 57g carbohydrates; 56.5g sugar; 0g fibre; 0.17g sodium

lemon syllabub with red fruits

SERVES 4

for the syllabub:

125ml dry white wine

60ml brandy

finely grated zest and juice of 1 lemon

1 tablespoon runny honey

300ml double cream

pinch of grated nutmeg

for the red fruits:

250g strawberries, hulled and quartered

225g raspberries

150g blackberries

100g redcurrants, stems removed and
   discarded

125ml Crème de Cassis liqueur

2 tablespoons Splenda granulated
   sweetener

1 tablespoon lemon juice

Syllabubs have been eaten in England for hundreds of years and this tangy lemon one makes a wonderful complement to the sweetness of the red fruits. Great on a hot summer's evening after a barbeque.

Place the wine, brandy, 1 teaspoon lemon zest, lemon juice and runny honey in a non-reactive bowl and leave overnight for the flavours to mingle and develop.

The next day, add the double cream and nutmeg and beat with a whisk until the syllabub holds its shape. Pour into a glass bowl and refrigerate.

In another glass bowl, combine all the fruits gently with the liqueur, sweetener and lemon juice. Leave for about 3 hours, turning the fruits from time to time, before serving.

Serve the syllabub and fruits in their separate bowls and allow your guests to combine or eat separately as they wish. A very refreshing combination.

Per serving: 589kcal; 3g protein; 46g fat; 22.6g saturated fat; 22g carbohydrates; 21.7g sugar; 4.1g fibre; 0.05g sodium

lime, lemongrass and mint jellies

SERVES 4

1 lemongrass stalk, cut into short
  lengths
a handful of fresh mint leaves
1½ tablespoons powdered gelatine
finely grated zest and juice of 2 limes
3 tablespoons Splenda granulated
  sweetener
4 tablespoons ginger, lemongrass or
  elderflower cordial
lime slices, to decorate

These sophisticated jellies are meant for adults – though children might like them too!

Bash the pieces of lemongrass with a rolling pin to bruise them, then put them into a saucepan with 6 of the mint leaves and 200ml water. Simmer gently for 15 minutes, or until the liquid has reduced by about half.

Strain the hot lemongrass-flavoured liquid through a sieve into a large measuring jug and stir in the powdered gelatine. Leave to dissolve for 5–6 minutes, stirring occasionally to give a completely clear liquid.

Stir the lime zest, lime juice and sweetener into the lemongrass liquid. Add the cordial, then pour in enough water to bring the level up to 700ml. Pour into 4 glasses, then transfer to the fridge to chill and set. This will take about 3 hours.

Serve the jellies decorated with the remaining mint leaves and the lime slices.

Per serving: 56kcal; 4g protein; 0g fat; 0g saturated fat; 11g carbohydrates; 10.3g sugar; 0g fibre; 0.02g sodium

melon and ginger granita

SERVES 6

500g Galia melon (weighed without
skin and seeds), cut into chunks
2 tablespoons lemon juice
3 pieces stem ginger in syrup, plus 3
tablespoons syrup from the jar
300ml unsweetened apple juice
6 tablespoons Splenda granulated
sweetener

**Ice cool and so refreshing, this sophisticated granita is perfect for a
hot summer's day.**

Put the melon chunks into a blender with the lemon juice, 1 piece of stem
ginger, apple juice and sweetener. Blend until very smooth. (You may have
to do this in batches.) Finely chop the remaining stem ginger and stir into the
melon purée.

Tip the mixture into an ice-cream maker and follow the manufacturer's
instructions to freeze the mixture. Alternatively, tip into a freezer container and
freeze for about 1 hour. Stir with a fork to break up the ice crystals, then freeze
again for another hour. Repeat the stirring, then freeze until solid.

Remove the container from the freezer about 25 minutes before you wish to
serve the granita – you can tell it's ready when you can break it up with a fork.
Scoop into chilled glasses or bowls and serve immediately.

Per serving: 43kcal; 0g protein; 0g fat; 0g saturated fat; 11g carbohydrates;
10.7g sugar; 0.3g fibre; 0.02g sodium

tiramisù

SERVES 6

3 eggs, separated

2 tablespoons Splenda granulated
sweetener

250g mascarpone cheese

4–5 tablespoons Tia Maria liqueur

300ml cold strong black coffee (real
coffee is best)

225g sponge fingers

dark chocolate (minimum 70% cocoa
solids), grated, to decorate

Melinda says: Tiramisù is my ultimate dinner party dessert. It's a classic Italian dish and with this recipe, it takes almost no time to prepare, which leaves me with more time to spend with my guests!

Place the egg yolks and sweetener into a bowl. Whisk thoroughly until the mixture lightens and thickens slightly, then stir in the mascarpone. Beat the egg whites until stiff and fold them in, a little at a time.

Mix the liqueur with the coffee and dip half the sponge fingers into the liquid to soak them. Use the soaked fingers to line the base of a shallow dish, then spoon over a generous half of the mascarpone mixture. Dip the remaining sponge fingers in the liquid and make another layer, finishing off with the remaining mascarpone mixture.

Chill for a few hours (longer if you can – the flavours will mature the longer you manage to leave it) and sprinkle with grated chocolate just before serving.

Per serving: 435kcal; 8g protein; 27g fat; 15.1g saturated fat; 37g carbohydrates; 24.1g sugar; 0.9g fibre; 0.11g sodium

blackcurrant fool

SERVES 4

450g fresh blackcurrants
2 tablespoons Splenda granulated
  sweetener
150ml double cream
150ml natural yogurt
4 sprigs fresh mint

The intense flavour of fresh blackcurrants is sublime and they are also full of goodness – bags of vitamin C (perhaps three times as much as in oranges) and antioxidants called anthocyanins, which give blackcurrants their deep, dark colour. For me they make the perfect fool.

Wash the blackcurrants and remove the stalks. You can do this easily by running a fork down them.

Put the blackcurrants and sweetener into a saucepan, add 50ml of water and bring gently to the boil. Simmer for around 15 minutes, stirring occasionally, until the fruit is well softened and the sweetener completely dissolved.

Push the blackcurrants through a mouli or blitz them in a liquidiser for a few seconds, then sieve them to remove the pips from the fruit. Set the purée aside to cool.

Beat the cream until it is good and thick, and then whisk in the yogurt, a spoonful at a time. Gently fold the creamy mixture into the fruit purée until roughly blended – you don't want to knock all the air out of it, and a little marbling looks pretty too.

Chill well in the fridge and serve in individual glasses, decorated with the sprigs of mint.

Per serving: 240kcal; 4g protein; 21g fat; 11.5g saturated fat; 11g carbohydrates; 11.1g sugar; 4g fibre; 0.04g sodium

tia maria mousse

SERVES 6

1 tablespoon powdered gelatine

7 tablespoons Splenda granulated
  sweetener

1 teaspoon coffee powder or granules

2 eggs, separated

4 tablespoons Tia Maria liqueur

150ml whipping cream

½ teaspoon cocoa powder

This light yet indulgent mousse ticks all the boxes for a yummy pudding.

Pour 150ml of very hot, but not boiling, water into a bowl and sprinkle over the powdered gelatine. Give it a stir, then leave to dissolve for about 5 minutes until you have a completely clear liquid.

Meanwhile, put 5 tablespoons of the sweetener into a small saucepan with the coffee powder or granules and 4 teaspoons of water. Heat gently for a few seconds until the sweetener and coffee have dissolved.

Whisk the egg whites in a grease-free bowl until stiff. Slowly add the coffee liquid, beating it in well.

Put the egg yolks, remaining 2 tablespoons of sweetener and the liqueur into a large heatproof bowl. Place the bowl over a saucepan of gently simmering water and whisk with a hand-held electric mixer until thick and frothy. This will take at least 5 minutes. Fold in the egg white mixture and dissolved gelatine.

Whip the cream until thick, then fold about two thirds of it through the mixture. Divide the mousse between six glasses and chill in the fridge until set – this will take about 2 hours. Just before serving, top the desserts with the remaining whipped cream and sprinkle with the cocoa powder.

Per serving: 166kcal; 4g protein; 12g fat; 6.7g saturated fat; 5g carbohydrates; 4.8g sugar; 0g fibre; 0.04g sodium

christmas cake

SERVES 20

1kg mixed dried fruit

100g glacé cherries, halved

150ml brandy or dark rum, plus 3
   tablespoons

175g butter, softened, plus extra for
   greasing

10 tablespoons Splenda granulated
   sweetener

4 eggs

2 tablespoons black treacle

finely grated zest and juice of 1 small
   orange

100g ground almonds

300g plain flour

¼ teaspoon salt

1 teaspoon mixed spice

for the icing:

4 tablespoons apricot baking glaze or
   sieved apricot jam

icing sugar, for dusting

500g marzipan

750g ready-rolled icing

Make this cake a couple of days before Christmas and use within ten days – it will not keep quite as long as a traditional cake.

The day before baking the cake, put the dried fruit, cherries and rum or brandy into a large bowl. Stir well and cover. Soak for 24 hours, stirring occasionally.

The next day, grease a 20cm round cake tin and line with a double layer of greaseproof paper. Preheat the oven to 150°C/300°F/gas mark 2. In a very large bowl, beat the butter and sweetener together until light and creamy. Beat in the eggs one by one, then stir in the treacle. Add the orange zest, juice and ground almonds. Sift in the flour, salt and mixed spice, then fold in using a large metal spoon. Stir in the soaked dried fruit, mixing thoroughly.

Tip into the cake tin and level with the back of a spoon. Bake for about 2¼ hours. After 2 hours, cover with a double layer of greaseproof paper to prevent it from getting too dark. To check whether the cake is done, insert a skewer into the middle of the cake – it should come out clean. If not, cook for a little longer.

Leave the tin on a wire rack to cool completely, then remove the tin. Spoon over the extra 3 tablespoons brandy or rum, letting it soak in. Warm the apricot glaze or jam, then brush it all over the cake. Dust your work surface with icing sugar and roll out half the marzipan into a long strip. Trim it to fit around the sides of the cake and place in position. Roll out the remaining marzipan into a circle and fit it on top of the cake. Cover with clingfilm and allow to harden for 24 hours.

The following day, dust your work surface and a rolling pin with icing sugar. Roll out the ready-rolled icing and continue to roll until it's large enough to cover the top and sides of the cake. Smooth the icing over the cake with your hands. Trim off any excess and decorate to your liking.

Per serving: 587kcal; 6g protein; 16g fat; 5.4g saturated fat; 105g carbohydrates; 93g sugar; 2.8g fibre; 0.15g sodium

everyday puddings

apple pie

SERVES 6

50g unsalted butter, plus extra for
greasing

1 large Bramley apple, peeled, cored
and sliced

4 dessert apples, peeled, cored and
sliced

3 tablespoons Splenda granulated
sweetener

10 cloves

1½ teaspoons mixed spice

2 tablespoons lemon juice

375g sweet shortcrust or puff pastry
flour, for dusting

1 egg, beaten

**This is a double crust apple pie that's best made on a metal pie plate so
the bottom has a chance to crisp up. If you don't have a metal pie plate,
use a small shallow pie dish and line the sides and top of the dish only.**

Preheat the oven to 200°C/400°F/gas mark 6, adding a baking sheet to heat
through. Grease a 22cm pie plate.

Melt half the butter in a large frying pan. Add the apples and sweetener and
cook gently for 5 minutes, stirring frequently, until the apples start to soften. Stir
in the spices and lemon juice and leave to cool.

Roll out half the pastry on a lightly floured surface and use to line the pie plate.
Scatter the apples and juices over the top, piling them up in the centre. Dot with
the remaining butter. Brush the edges of the pastry with the beaten egg.

Roll out the remaining pastry and use to cover the pie. Press the edges together
with the tines of a fork to seal. Trim off any excess pastry and use to decorate
if desired. Make a few slashes in the top with a sharp knife – this will allow the
steam to escape. Brush the top with more beaten egg and bake in the oven for
35–40 minutes until pale golden.

Per serving: 348kcal; 4g protein; 22g fat; 10.3g saturated fat; 36g carbohydrates;
13g sugar; 1.8g fibre; 0.2g sodium

rhubarb free-form pie

SERVES 6

50g cold butter, cut into cubes, plus
   extra for greasing
225g plain flour, plus extra for dusting
pinch of salt
50g vegetable fat (for pastry-making),
   cut into cubes
1 egg, beaten
25g ground semolina or instant polenta
700g rhubarb, trimmed and chopped
8 tablespoons Splenda granulated
   sweetener

In this pie the rhubarb is simply encased in a loosely formed pastry crust – meaning you don't have to be too precise with your rolling and measuring.

Preheat the oven to 190°C/375°F/gas mark 5. Lightly grease a large baking tray with a little butter.

Sift the flour and salt into a bowl. Add the butter and vegetable fat and rub together with your fingertips until the mixture resembles fine breadcrumbs. Add just enough cold water to make a smooth, but not sticky, dough. Wrap in clingfilm and refrigerate for 10–15 minutes.

Roll out the pastry on a lightly floured surface to form a circle measuring about 35cm in diameter. Lift carefully onto the baking tray. Brush the surface with beaten egg and sprinkle the semolina or polenta over the middle, to within 8cm of the edge. This will to soak up the juices from the fruit, helping to prevent the pastry base from getting soggy.

Mix the rhubarb and sweetener together, then pile on top of the semolina or polenta. Draw up the edges of the pastry around the fruit, overlapping where necessary and pressing together. Don't expect the pastry to cover the fruit.

Brush the pastry again with beaten egg. Bake on the middle shelf for 25–30 minutes, until golden brown. Serve warm with custard, ice cream or natural yogurt.

Per serving: 307kcal; 6g protein; 17g fat; 6.8g saturated fat; 35g carbohydrates; 3.5g sugar; 2.9g fibre; 0.17g sodium

bananas in citrus rum sauce

SERVES 4

40g butter

6 bananas (not too ripe), thickly sliced

finely grated zest and juice of 1 large orange

2 tablespoons Splenda granulated sweetener

50g raisins or sultanas

3 tablespoons rum or brandy

1–2 tablespoons flaked almonds, toasted

For a quick, delicious pudding, this recipe comes up trumps!

Melt the butter in a large frying pan and add the bananas. Cook them for a minute or so over a medium heat to warm them through. Make sure you don't overcook them, or else they will go soggy.

Add 1 teaspoon orange zest, the orange juice, sweetener and raisins or sultanas to the pan. Cook over a low heat, stirring gently, for 1 minute. Remove the pan from the heat and stir in the rum or brandy, then place back on the heat to let the sauce bubble for a moment or two. Scatter the flaked almonds on top, then serve at once.

Per serving: 296kcal; 3g protein; 10g fat; 5.5g saturated fat; 46g carbohydrates; 42.4g sugar; 2.1g fibre; 0.07g sodium

greek lemon puddings

SERVES 4

300g soft cheese

finely grated zest of 1 large lemon

4 tablespoons Splenda granulated
   sweetener

250g 0% fat Greek yogurt

1 teaspoon vanilla extract

2 large eggs, beaten

175g fresh or thawed frozen
   raspberries

Make these delightful puddings in individual flan dishes or ramekins – it makes serving them much easier.

Preheat the oven to 180°C/350°F/gas mark 4.

Beat the soft cheese and lemon zest together until combined, then beat in the sweetener, yogurt and vanilla extract. Strain the beaten eggs through a sieve into the cheese mixture and beat well.

Pour the mixture into four individual flan or ramekin dishes. Stand the dishes in a large, deep roasting pan and pour in enough warm water to come halfway up their sides. Transfer carefully to the oven and bake for 25–30 minutes, until set.

Serve the puddings warm or chilled, topped with the raspberries.

Per serving: 182kcal; 19g protein; 8g fat; 3.4g saturated fat; 10g carbohydrates; 8.2g sugar; 1.4g fibre; 0.39g sodium

kiwi and grape cheesecake layer

SERVES 4

8 digestive biscuits, crushed

4 tablespoons marsala or sweet sherry

2 kiwis, peeled and sliced

250g seedless grapes, halved

200g soft cheese

300g Greek-style natural yogurt

2 tablespoons Splenda granulated
sweetener

½ teaspoon vanilla extract

You won't believe how delicious this simple, layered dessert tastes – so why not make it to find out?

Divide half the digestive biscuit crumbs over four individual glasses. Sprinkle 1 tablespoon of marsala or sherry evenly over each one.

Mix the kiwi slices with the grapes and spoon half the fruit into the glasses.

Beat the soft cheese with a wooden spoon until creamy and soft, then mix in the yogurt, sweetener and vanilla extract. Spoon this mixture into the glasses, on top of the fruit.

Sprinkle over the remaining biscuit crumbs, followed by the rest of the fruit. Cover and chill until ready to serve.

Per serving: 359kcal; 13g protein; 16g fat; 8.3g saturated fat; 40g carbohydrates; 22.3g sugar; 1.4g fibre; 0.44g sodium

frozen berry yogurt

SERVES 8

450g frozen summer berries or
  raspberries
10 tablespoons Splenda granulated
  sweetener
500g Greek-style natural yogurt
2 teaspoons vanilla extract

**Frozen summer fruits are available in most supermarkets and great for
this easy dessert.**

Put the frozen berries into a blender or food processor. Add the sweetener,
yogurt and vanilla extract and blend for about 20 seconds until combined.

Tip the mixture into an ice-cream maker and follow the manufacturer's
instructions to freeze. Alternatively, tip the mixture into a rigid freezer container
and freeze for about 1 hour. Remove and stir with a fork to break up the ice
crystals. Repeat this every hour, twice more, then freeze the mixture until solid.

Remove the container from the freezer about 30 minutes before serving to
allow the mixture to soften a little. Scoop into chilled glasses and serve.

Per serving: 100kcal; 5g protein; 6g fat; 3.6g saturated fat; 8g carbohydrates;
7.7g sugar; 1.5g fibre; 0.05g sodium

coffee panna cotta

SERVES 6

6 sheets leaf gelatine (10g in total)
6 tablespoons Baileys liqueur
200g soft cheese
1 teaspoon vanilla extract
300ml milk
100ml single cream
150ml strong black coffee
2 tablespoons Splenda granulated
    sweetener

The liqueur gives this lovely pudding some added oomph!

Use a pair of scissors to snip the sheets of leaf gelatine into a shallow bowl. Spoon the liqueur over them and leave for 5 minutes, until slightly softened.

Meanwhile, put the soft cheese, vanilla extract and 2 tablespoons of the milk into a saucepan and whisk until smooth. Stir in the remaining milk and the single cream to give a smooth liquid. Heat gently, stirring all the time, until hot but not boiling. Remove from the heat and add the gelatine and liqueur. Stir until the gelatine has dissolved, then mix in the coffee and sweetener.

Wet the insides of six 150ml moulds or ramekin dishes. Fill with the panna cotta mixture. Chill for about 3–4 hours, or overnight, until set.

To serve, dip the moulds briefly into hot water and turn out onto pretty plates.

Per serving: 218kcal; 7g protein; 17g fat; 9g saturated fat; 7g carbohydrates; 7.1g sugar; 0g fibre; 0.16g sodium

rhubarb and ginger fool

SERVES 4

550g rhubarb, trimmed and cut into
2.5cm pieces

8 tablespoons Splenda granulated
sweetener

2 pieces stem ginger in syrup, plus 2
tablespoons syrup from the jar

150g mascarpone cheese

4 tablespoons natural Greek-style
yogurt

4 Ginger Nuts biscuits, roughly crushed

Simple flavours combine to make an easy, sensational pudding.

Put the rhubarb and sweetener into a large, shallow pan. Add 4 tablespoons of water and the stem ginger syrup. Place on the heat and simmer gently, without a lid, for 6–8 minutes, until the rhubarb is tender but not mushy. Leave to cool.

Meanwhile, chop 1 piece of stem ginger and finely slice the other.

Divide half the rhubarb, with some of the juice from the pan, between four serving glasses.

Mix the remaining rhubarb, without its juice, with the mascarpone cheese and yogurt. Fold in the chopped stem ginger and most of the crushed biscuits. Spoon the mixture into the serving glasses.

To decorate the desserts, sprinkle the reserved crushed biscuits and slices of stem ginger over the top, then chill until ready to serve.

Per serving: 292kcal; 4g protein; 20g fat; 12.2g saturated fat; 25g carbohydrates; 19.8g sugar; 2.3g fibre; 0.09g sodium

strawberry soufflé omelette

SERVES 2

225g strawberries, hulled and halved

1 tablespoon lemon juice

3 tablespoons Splenda granulated
   sweetener

4 eggs, separated

1 teaspoon vanilla extract

10g butter

Soufflé omelettes may sound quite special, yet they are a quick and easy way to produce a nutritious pudding.

Put the strawberries into a small saucepan. Add the lemon juice, half the sweetener and 2 tablespoons of water. Heat gently until the fruit has softened slightly – this will take about 2 minutes. Turn the heat to very low.

Preheat the grill to hot. In a large, grease-free bowl, whisk the egg whites until they hold their shape. In a separate bowl, beat the egg yolks with the remaining sweetener and the vanilla extract. Fold the egg yolk mixture into the egg whites using a large metal spoon.

Melt half the butter in a medium-sized non-stick omelette pan or frying pan. Add half the egg mixture and cook for about a minute until the bottom of the soufflé has set. Place the pan under the grill for a few moments until the top has set and browned a little.

Slide onto a warm plate, fill with half the strawberries and fold double. Keep warm whilst you make the second omelette, then serve at once.

Per serving: 232kcal; 13g protein; 15g fat; 5.6g saturated fat; 10g carbohydrates; 10.4g sugar; 1.2g fibre; 0.18g sodium

french toast with fresh berry sauce

SERVES 2

for the french toast:

1 egg

150ml milk

1 teaspoon vanilla extract

1 tablespoon Splenda granulated
sweetener

2 thick slices white bread, crusts
removed

25g butter

for the fresh berry sauce:

75g blueberries

75g raspberries

75g strawberries, hulled and sliced

1 tablespoon Splenda granulated
sweetener

Try this recipe for a fast, easy dessert or enjoy it as a satisfying, nutritious start to the day.

In a large shallow bowl, beat together the egg, milk, vanilla extract and sweetener. Cut each slice of bread in half diagonally and add the pieces of bread to the egg mixture. Leave them to soak for about 5 minutes, turning them once.

Melt the butter in a large frying pan. Add the soaked bread and fry gently for 1–2 minutes until set and golden brown. Turn over the pieces and cook them on the other side for a further 1–2 minutes.

Meanwhile, put the berries and remaining sweetener into a saucepan with 2 tablespoons water. Heat and simmer gently for 2–3 minutes. Serve with the hot French toast.

Per serving: 302kcal; 10g protein; 15g fat; 8.2g saturated fat; 33g carbohydrates; 14g sugar; 2.6g fibre; 0.35g sodium

fruity clafoutis

SERVES 4

1 teaspoon butter

1 apple, peeled, cored and chopped

1 tablespoon lemon juice

4 ready-to-eat dried apricots, roughly
  chopped

3 plums, stoned and quartered

40g sultanas

2 eggs

225ml milk

3 tablespoons Splenda granulated
  sweetener

1 tablespoon plain flour

2–3 drops vanilla extract

**Clafoutis, a traditional French pudding made with a light batter, is
delicious with this selection of orchard fruits.**

Preheat the oven to 180°C/350°F/gas mark 4. Grease a 1.2 litre shallow baking
dish with the butter.

Mix together the apple, lemon juice, apricots, plums and sultanas. Tip them into
the baking dish and spread out in an even layer.

Using a wire whisk, beat together the eggs, milk, sweetener, flour and vanilla
extract to make a smooth batter. Pour over the fruit layer and place in the oven.

Bake for 35–40 minutes until set and golden. Serve hot with single cream or
natural yogurt.

Per serving: 159kcal; 6g protein; 5g fat; 2g saturated fat; 24g carbohydrates;
20.8g sugar; 1.9g fibre; 0.07g sodium

hot mango and pineapple meringue pudding

SERVES 4

227g tin pineapple pieces in natural juice

3 tablespoons cornflour

2 large eggs, separated

450ml semi-skimmed milk

1 teaspoon vanilla extract

4 tablespoons Splenda granulated sweetener

1 small mango, peeled, stoned and chopped

This easy pudding looks fabulous and tastes divine – you must try it!

Preheat the oven to 190°C/375°C/gas mark 5.

Drain the pineapple juice into a medium-sized non-stick saucepan. Blend in the cornflour, then stir in the egg yolks, milk and vanilla extract. Heat, stirring all the time with a small whisk or wooden spoon, until the mixture boils and thickens.

Remove the pan from the heat and stir in half the sweetener. Add the pineapple pieces and chopped mango and stir well.

Spoon the mixture into a 1.2 litre baking dish or four individual dishes. Place on a baking tray and bake for 5 minutes whilst preparing the meringue topping.

Whisk the egg whites in a grease-free bowl until they hold their shape. Add the remaining sweetener and whisk again until the meringue is stiff. Pile onto the hot pudding and bake for a further 4–5 minutes until billowy and golden brown.

Per serving: 205kcal; 8g protein; 5g fat; 2g saturated fat; 33g carbohydrates; 22.1g sugar; 1.8g fibre; 0.1g sodium

mango and yogurt fool

SERVES 4

600g Greek-style yogurt
1 tablespoon grated fresh ginger (and
   the juices)
1 teaspoon ground cardamom
2 mangoes, peeled and stoned
150ml double cream
1 tablespoon Splenda granulated
   sweetener
½ teaspoon vanilla extract
strips of orange zest, to decorate

The combination of yogurt and mango works surprisingly well in this rich and tasty fool. Fools are found in old English cookery books, yet the name Fool comes from *fouler*, French for 'to crush'. The fruit in this fool is soft, so it doesn't need cooking before it goes into the dish.

Combine the yogurt with the ginger and its juices (grating the ginger over a bowl to catch them). Add in the ground cardamom.

Finely dice one of the mangoes and set it aside. Cut the flesh off the other and purée it in a liquidiser. For an extra smooth purée, pass it through a fine plastic sieve. Mix the diced mango and the purée into the yogurt.

Whip the cream with the sweetener and vanilla extract until it forms soft peaks. Fold the cream into the mango yogurt and spoon the mixture into glasses. Refrigerate until required.

Blanch the strips of orange zest quickly in boiling water for 1–2 minutes and leave to cool. Use these to decorate the fool. Serve in pretty individual glasses, well chilled.

Per serving: 442kcal; 11g protein; 34g fat; 19.9g saturated fat; 24g carbohydrates; 22.4g sugar; 3.4g fibre; 0.12g sodium

plum, fig and blueberry fruit salad

SERVES 4

1 small unwaxed lemon

1 cinnamon stick

4 tablespoons Splenda granulated
  sweetener

300g plums, halved and stoned

200g blueberries

4 fresh figs, quartered

Fruit salads are delicious and so good for you – and this one combines some great flavours.

Cut a wide strip of lemon zest from the lemon using a speed peeler and put into a saucepan. Squeeze the lemon and add the juice to the pan with the cinnamon stick, sweetener and 200ml of water. Place on the heat and simmer gently for 2 minutes.

Add the plums to the saucepan and simmer gently for a further 5–6 minutes, until tender. Remove the saucepan from the heat and add the blueberries. Cool for 10 minutes, then discard the strip of lemon zest and the cinnamon stick.

Add the figs to the plum mixture, stir everything together gently, then serve barely warm or chilled.

Per serving: 72kcal; 1g protein; 0g fat; 0g saturated fat; 17g carbohydrates; 16.8g sugar; 2.9g fibre; 0g sodium

raspberry cranachan

SERVES 4

50g rolled oats
225g raspberries
300ml double cream
2 tablespoons Splenda granulated
  sweetener

Cranachan is a luxury version of the Scottish crowdie, developed for eating at harvest festivals and using cream instead of water of buttermilk. For a lighter version, replace the whipped cream with a 500g pot of Greek-style yogurt.

Preheat the grill. Sprinkle the rolled oats onto a baking tray and spread them out evenly. Carefully toast them until they are light brown – this will take 2–3 minutes. Keep a close eye on them to make sure that they don't burn. Cool completely.

Put half the raspberries into a bowl. Use a fork or potato masher to crush them lightly. Put the remaining whole raspberries into four serving glasses, reserving some for decoration.

In a large chilled mixing bowl, whip the double cream until thick. Tip in the crushed raspberries and toasted oats. Add the sweetener and stir together gently. There's no need to mix everything thoroughly – a random, marbled effect will look great.

Spoon the cream mixture into the serving glasses and decorate with the reserved raspberries. Cover and chill until ready to serve.

Per serving: 436kcal; 4g protein; 41g fat; 22.8g saturated fat; 13g carbohydrates; 4.6g sugar; 2.7g fibre; 0.02g sodium

rice pudding

SERVES 4

50g pudding rice
25g skimmed milk powder
2 tablespoons Splenda granulated
  sweetener
600ml semi-skimmed milk
1 teaspoon ground nutmeg
strawberry jam, to serve

Melinda says: This recipe is a great everyday dish. You can keep it simple, or follow my tip for extra flavour by adding a spoonful of strawberry conserve on top.

Preheat the oven to 150°C/300°F/gas mark 2.

Place the rice, skimmed milk powder, sweetener and milk in a 1 litre ovenproof dish. Mix together and then smooth out evenly.

Sprinkle over half the ground nutmeg and place on the middle shelf of the oven.

Bake for 45 minutes, then remove the dish from the oven and either stir in the skin that has formed on top, or remove it.

Sprinkle over the remaining nutmeg and return to the oven.

Bake for a further 45 minutes until the top is golden brown, the rice is soft and most of the liquid has been absorbed. Serve hot or cold with a few teaspoons of strawberry jam.

Per serving: 588kcal; 55g protein; 1g fat; 0.6g saturated fat; 95g carbohydrates; 85.4g sugar; 0g fibre; 0.83g sodium

apricot fool

SERVES 4

500g fresh apricots, halved and stoned
1 tablespoon Splenda granulated
   sweetener
350ml double cream
mint leaves, to decorate (optional)

The flavour of a warm, ripe apricot picked off a tree in the sunshine stays with you for life! Combined into a fool, this makes a very pleasing pudding.

Place the apricot halves into a saucepan with the sweetener and 50ml of water. Bring to simmering point over a gentle heat, and continue cooking for about 5 minutes until the apricots are just softening.

The sweetness of this dish depends on how ripe the fruit is and how sweet you like it, so taste and add some more sweetener according to taste.

Push the apricots through a mouli or blitz them for 30 seconds in a liquidiser. Set aside to cool thoroughly.

Whisk the double cream until it forms soft peaks. Fold in the apricot purée. Serve well chilled and decorate with a few mint leaves if you like.

Per serving: 475kcal; 3g protein; 47g fat; 26.4g saturated fat; 11g carbohydrates; 10.8g sugar; 2.1g fibre; 0.02g sodium

scotch pancakes with blueberries

MAKES 10

110g plain flour

1 teaspoon baking powder

1 tablespoon Splenda granulated
sweetener

1 egg

150ml semi-skimmed milk

20g lightly salted butter, melted

150g fresh or frozen blueberries

1 tablespoon maple syrup

1 tablespoon sunflower oil

These pancakes are perfect for a leisurely breakfast or late morning snack. Serve as they are or topped with spoonfuls of crème fraîche or Greek yogurt.

Mix together the flour, baking powder and sweetener in a bowl. Make a well in the centre and break in the egg. Add a little of the milk and whisk with the egg, gradually incorporating the flour to make a smooth batter. Add the remaining milk and the butter and mix until smooth.

Put the blueberries and maple syrup in a small saucepan and heat gently until the blueberry juices start to run. Transfer to a small serving bowl.

Heat a dash of the oil in a large, heavy-based frying pan. Pour a little of the batter into the pan so it spreads to a pancake about 7.5cm in diameter. Pour in several more rounds, leaving a little space between each and cook gently for 1 minute or until golden on the underside. Turn the pancakes with a palette knife and cook for a further minute. Remove to a warmed plate and repeat with the remaining batter, adding more oil when the pan gets dry.

Pile the pancakes onto serving plates and sprinkle with a little more sweetener if you like. Serve with the blueberries.

Per serving: 87kcal; 2g protein; 4g fat; 1.5g saturated fat; 12g carbohydrates; 3.1g sugar; 0.6g fibre; 0.09g sodium

warm berries with sabayon sauce

SERVES 4

225g blueberries

3 tablespoons Splenda granulated
   sweetener

225g strawberries, hulled and halved

225g raspberries

2 egg yolks

50ml white grape juice or apple juice

50ml white wine

This simple summer pudding tastes sensational with its frothy white wine sauce.

Put the blueberries, 1 tablespoon sweetener and 3 tablespoons cold water into a saucepan. Heat gently for 2–3 minutes until the juice begins to run from the fruit. Cool slightly, then mix gently with the strawberries and raspberries.

Using a hand-held electric mixer, whisk the egg yolks with the remaining sweetener in a large heatproof bowl until very pale in colour and light in texture. Add the grape or apple juice and white wine and continue to whisk, standing the bowl over a saucepan of gently simmering water until the sauce thickens. Remove from the heat and whisk for a further 30 seconds or so.

Divide the fruit between individual serving dishes and spoon the sauce on top.

Per serving: 99kcal; 3g protein; 4g fat; 0.9g saturated fat; 13g carbohydrates; 12.9g sugar; 3g fibre; 0.01g sodium

family favourites

deep-filled pear pie with crème anglaise

SERVES 6

225g plain flour, plus extra for dusting
pinch of salt
50g white vegetable fat, diced
50g cold butter, diced
1 egg, beaten
juice of 1 lemon
750g not too ripe pears
5 tablespoons Splenda granulated
   sweetener

for the crème anglaise:
300ml whole milk
300ml single cream
1 vanilla pod, split open lengthways
4 large organic egg yolks
2 tablespoons Splenda granulated
   sweetener

Put the flour and salt into a bowl. Add the vegetable fat and butter and rub in with your fingertips until the mixture looks like fine breadcrumbs. Add just enough cold water to make a soft, but not sticky dough. Knead lightly for a few moments until smooth, then wrap in clingfilm and chill for 10 minutes.

Preheat the oven to 200°C/400°C/gas mark 6. Divide the pastry into two equal pieces. Roll out each piece on a lightly floured work surface into a circle with a diameter of 25cm. Use one circle to line a 23cm pie plate. Brush the base with a little beaten egg.

Squeeze the lemon juice into a bowl. Peel, core and slice the pears, and place into the bowl with the sweetener. Toss together and tip into the pie dish. Brush the edges of the pastry with a little water, then cover with the second pastry circle, pressing the edges together to seal. Trim with a sharp knife, then brush the surface with beaten egg.

Bake in the oven for 25–30 minutes, until the pastry is golden brown. Meanwhile, make the crème anglaise. Place the milk, cream and vanilla pod in a heavy based saucepan and slowly bring to the boil. Remove from the heat and leave to infuse for 15 minutes.

Whisk the egg yolks with the sweetener in a bowl. Pour the cream mixture over the yolks, whisking well. Lift out the vanilla pod and, with a teaspoon, scrape the seeds back into the custard. Clean the saucepan and return the mixture to the pan. Cook very gently over the lowest heat, stirring constantly until the sauce is thick enough to coat the back of the spoon. This will take about 8–10 minutes. Pour into a serving jug.

Remove the pie from the oven and leave to cool for a few minutes. Serve with the crème anglaise.

Per serving: 499kcal; 11g protein; 33g fat; 14.9g saturated fat; 44g carbohydrates; 14.9g sugar; 2.5g fibre; 0.24g sodium

panettone and clementine bread and butter pudding

SERVES 6

40g butter

6 slices (about 350g) panettone or light
   fruit bread

3 clementines, peeled and thinly sliced

3 eggs

600ml semi-skimmed milk

150ml single cream

3 tablespoons Splenda granulated
   sweetener

1 teaspoon vanilla extract

pinch of ground nutmeg

Try this classic favourite with a twist – made with Italian panettone or light fruit bread and sliced clementines. It's truly delicious.

Use a little of the butter to grease a 1.5 litre baking dish. Spread the remaining butter over the slices of panettone or fruit bread. Cut them into triangles, then lay them in the dish, overlapping them to fit. Tuck the clementine slices in amongst the bread.

Beat together the eggs, milk, single cream, sweetener and vanilla extract. Pour into the dish, over the bread. Cover with clingfilm and leave for at least 30 minutes. If you want to cook the pudding later, refrigerate until required.

Preheat the oven to 180°C/350°F/gas mark 4.

Sprinkle the surface of the pudding with the ground nutmeg. Bake in the oven for 30–35 minutes until puffed up and golden brown. Cool for a few minutes, then serve.

Per serving: 422kcal; 11g protein; 24g fat; 11.9g saturated fat; 42g carbohydrates; 28.8g sugar; 1.1g fibre; 0.24g sodium

apple and blackberry charlotte

SERVES 4

750g baking apples, peeled, cored and chopped
finely grated zest and juice of 1 orange
pinch of ground cinnamon
200g blackberries
4-5 tablespoons Splenda granulated sweetener
50g butter, melted
7 slices white bread, crusts removed

Remind yourself just how good this traditional favourite tastes!

Preheat the oven to 180°C/350°F/gas mark 4.

Put the apples into a saucepan with the orange zest, orange juice and cinnamon. Add 5 tablespoons of water, then simmer without a lid until the apples are tender – this will take about 10 minutes. Stir in the blackberries, then sweeten to taste with the sweetener.

Brush a 15cm straight-sided baking dish or cake tin with melted butter. Brush the rest of the butter over the slices of bread. Place one slice in the base of the dish or tin, reserve one for the top, then fit the rest of the slices around the sides, easing them into place and cutting them to fit so that there are no spaces.

Spoon the apple and blackberry mixture into the lined baking dish and place the remaining slice of bread on top, folding the bread around the sides over to enclose the filling. Bake for 30–35 minutes. Cool for a few minutes, then serve.

Per serving: 299kcal; 5g protein; 12g fat; 6.7g saturated fat; 46g carbohydrates; 23.3g sugar; 5.3g fibre; 0.33g sodium

apple fritters

SERVES 4

for the batter:
110g plain flour
20g butter, melted
1 egg yolk, plus 2 egg whites
½ tablespoon Splenda granulated
   sweetener
grated zest of 1 lemon
3 tablespoons dark rum, plus extra for
   serving
½ teaspoon salt

vegetable oil, for frying
450g Cox's apples, cored and peeled
icing sugar, for dusting (optional)

This is something I used to have when I was a child. It brings back memories of all of us sitting around the table as a family. In our household, puddings were served daily – but those were the days when kids got much more exercise than today, just by playing outside.

Start by making the batter: beat together the flour, butter, 1 egg yolk, sweetener, lemon zest, rum, salt and 3 tablespoons of water. Leave the mixture to stand in the fridge for 30 minutes.

Just before you're ready to fry your fritters, whisk the egg whites in a grease-free bowl until they hold their shape, and fold into the mixture.

Fill a deep pan or deep fat fryer with vegetable oil and heat until hot.

Cut each apple into six wedges. Dip the wedges into the batter and fry a few at a time in the hot oil until nicely browned. Repeat until all are fried. Drain well on kitchen paper.

Sprinkle the fritters with a few drops of rum and dust them with icing sugar if you like.

Per serving: 358kcal; 6g protein; 20g fat; 4.9g saturated fat; 34g carbohydrates; 13.4g sugar; 3.1g fibre; 0.32g sodium

pumpkin pie

SERVES 6

1 x 23cm shortcrust pastry case

500g peeled and deseeded pumpkin, cut
   into 2.5cm chunks

3 eggs

2 tablespoons brown sugar

2 tablespoons Splenda granulated
   sweetener

1½ teaspoons ground cinnamon

1 teaspoon ground ginger

½ teaspoon allspice

½ teaspoon ground cloves

¼ teaspoon ground cardamom

pinch of sea salt

thick natural yogurt, to decorate

Melinda says: This is one of my all time favourite pies. The mix of spices and flavours is just so comforting during the colder months.

Preheat the oven to 190°C/375°F/gas mark 5. Prick the pastry case with a fork and line with a large piece of greaseproof paper. Fill the paper with a single layer of baking beans or dried pulses, then bake for 10–15 minutes. Lift out the greaseproof paper and beans.

Turn the oven temperature up to 220°C/425°F/gas mark 7.

To make the filling, steam the pumpkin until softened, then place in a coarse sieve and press lightly to extract any excess water. Mash it into a purée.

In a large bowl, beat the eggs, sugar and sweetener together until light and frothy. Add the mashed pumpkin, all the spices and the salt and blend into the egg mixture, stirring thoroughly.

Fill the pastry case and level the top of the filling roughly. Cook in the oven for around 8–10 minutes, then reduce the oven temperature to 160°C/325°F/gas mark 3 and continue cooking for another 30 minutes or until the filling is set. To check that the pie is cooked on the inside, insert a skewer into the centre and, if it comes out clean, the filling is cooked. Remove from the oven and allow to cool.

Spread the cake with the yogurt and sprinkle with a little extra cinnamon if you like. Keep in the fridge.

Per serving: 244kcal; 6g protein; 13g fat; 3.9g saturated fat; 27g carbohydrates; 10.6g sugar; 1.4g fibre; 0.25g sodium

lemon meringue pie

SERVES 6

1 x 20cm sweet pastry case
3 tablespoons cornflour
finely grated zest and juice of 2 large
  lemons
5 tablespoons Splenda granulated
  sweetener
2 large eggs, separated

Make a quick version of this popular dessert by using a shop-bought pastry case – though of course you could make your own, if you prefer.

Preheat the oven to 180°C/350°F/gas mark 4. Place the pastry case onto a baking tray.

In a small non-stick saucepan, blend the cornflour with 200ml cold water. Add the lemon zest and juice and bring to the boil, stirring constantly until the mixture thickens. Remove from the heat and stir in 4 tablespoons of sweetener. Cool for about 10 minutes, stirring often to prevent a skin from forming.

Mix the egg yolks into the lemon mixture, then pour into the pastry case. Bake in the oven for 12–15 minutes, until set.

Whisk the egg whites in a grease-free bowl until they hold their shape. Add the remaining sweetener and whisk again until you have a thick, glossy meringue.

Spread the meringue over the lemon filling and return to the oven for 5–6 minutes, until golden brown.

Per serving: 245kcal; 4g protein; 14g fat; 4.6g saturated fat; 27g carbohydrates; 5.2g sugar; 0.7g fibre; 0.11g sodium

plum muesli crumble with custard

SERVES 4

750g red plums, quartered and stoned
8 tablespoons Splenda granulated
   sweetener
2 tablespoons orange juice
50g butter
150g muesli
75g marzipan, coarsely grated

for the custard:
2 tablespoons custard powder
600ml semi-skimmed milk
2–3 tablespoons Splenda granulated
   sweetener

This recipe uses a very clever crumble topping, simply made by mixing good-quality muesli with melted butter and some grated marzipan. The flavour and texture are amazing.

Preheat the oven to 190°C/375°F/gas mark 5.

Put the plums into a baking dish and sprinkle with 6 tablespoons of sweetener and the orange juice. Toss to coat, then bake in the oven for 15 minutes while you prepare the topping.

Melt the butter and mix in the muesli, the remaining sweetener and the grated marzipan. Remove the baking dish from the oven and sprinkle the muesli topping over the plums in an even layer.

Place back in the oven and bake for 10–15 minutes, until the plums are tender and the topping is crunchy and golden brown.

To make the custard, put the custard powder into a saucepan with 4 tablespoons of the milk and stir until blended. Add the remaining milk, then heat, stirring constantly until smooth and thickened. Stir in sweetener to taste, and serve with the crumble.

Per serving: 489kcal; 11g protein; 18g fat; 8.6g saturated fat; 76g carbohydrates; 51.9g sugar; 6.1g fibre; 0.32g sodium

orange and sultana semolina puddings

SERVES 2

40g ground semolina
450ml semi-skimmed milk
25g sultanas or raisins
2 tablespoons Splenda granulated
  sweetener
½ teaspoon vanilla extract
pinch ground nutmeg or cinnamon
2 oranges
2 eggs, beaten

I've given this classic milk pudding a new interpretation.

Preheat the oven to 190°C/375°F/gas mark 5. Put the semolina into a saucepan and blend in the milk. Heat, stirring constantly, until thickened and smooth. Cook gently for a further 2–3 minutes, then remove from the heat.

Add the sultanas or raisins, sweetener, vanilla extract and ground nutmeg or cinnamon to the semolina and grate over the zest of 1 orange, using a fine grater. Squeeze the zested orange over the pan and stir together. Taste, adding a little extra sweetener if you like. Stir in the eggs and divide between two individual heatproof dishes. Bake in the oven for 10 minutes, or until just set.

Meanwhile, peel the remaining orange and cut into slices with a sharp, serrated knife.

Arrange the orange slices over the surface of the baked puddings. Bake for a further 5–6 minutes, until golden brown. Serve at once.

Per serving: 346kcal; 18g protein; 10g fat; 3.9g saturated fat; 48g carbohydrates; 32.2g sugar; 2.1g fibre; 0.18g sodium

gooseberry and elderflower compôte

SERVES 6

5 elderflower heads
2 tablespoons Splenda granulated
  sweetener
675g gooseberries, topped and tailed

Gooseberries can be readily found in farmers' markets throughout early summer and one is never far away from an elderflower bush in the British Isles, even in the cities, so finding these delicate and fragrant flowers should not be a problem!

Tie the elderflower heads together with a piece of string.

Put 300ml of water into a saucepan and stir in the sweetener. Add the gooseberries and elderflower heads. Simmer for about 15 minutes or until the gooseberries are cooked. Remove and discard the elderflowers.

Eat the gooseberry and elderflower compôte hot or cold. Try serving it with cream or ice cream. To make into a 'fool', fold in 150ml lightly whipped cream or a mixture of cream and custard.

Per serving: 40kcal; 1g protein; 0g fat; 0g saturated fat; 8g carbohydrates; 8.2g sugar; 2.7g fibre; 0g sodium

crunchy granola and raspberry pudding

SERVES 4

for the granola:

175g unsalted butter, cut into cubes, plus extra for greasing

225g rolled oats

4 tablespoons flaked almonds

2 tablespoons unsalted macadamia nuts, chopped

2 tablespoons hazelnuts, skins removed and roughly chopped

2 tablespoons brazil nuts, roughly chopped

2 tablespoons Splenda granulated sweetener

2 teaspoons grated orange zest

pinch of grated nutmeg

pinch of ground cloves

pinch of ground cinnamon

3 tablespoons golden syrup

25g dried apricots, finely diced

25g dates, finely diced

25g dried cherries

25g sultanas

25g Greek-style yogurt

250g fresh raspberries

It's lovely to make your own granola, and it can be used in so many ways – in this pudding, over your breakfast yogurt or even as a crunchy, nutritious snack. You'll be happy to find you have some leftovers after you've made this recipe...

Preheat the oven to 160°C/325°F/gas mark 3. Lightly grease two shallow oven trays with a little butter.

First of all, make the granola. Mix the rolled oats, nuts, sweetener, orange zest and spices together. Melt the butter and golden syrup in a large saucepan. Add the oat mixture and combine well. Pour this into the prepared tray. Pat the mix down and bake in the oven for 15–20 minutes.

Remove from the oven, place the second buttered tray over the hot tray and invert. Pat the granola down firmly again and return to the oven for a further 20–25 minutes or until golden brown.

Leave the granola to cool completely. Once cool, the granola will have become brittle. Break into small chunks and weigh out 225g for the pudding. (You'll have some leftovers that can be stored in an airtight container.)

Fold the granola and dried fruits into the yogurt. Scoop into a glass bowl, top with the fresh raspberries and serve.

Per serving: 388kcal; 6g protein; 24g fat; 10.8g saturated fat; 38g carbohydrates; 23.4g sugar; 5g fibre; 0.03g sodium

yorkshire curd tart

SERVES 6

for the pastry:
175g plain flour
pinch of salt
40g cold butter, cut into cubes, plus
  extra for greasing
40g vegetable fat (for pastry-making),
  cut into cubes
2 teaspoons Splenda granulated
  sweetener

for the filling:
2 eggs
4 tablespoons single cream
225g natural cottage cheese
3 tablespoons Splenda granulated
  sweetener
½ teaspoon vanilla extract
50g currants
finely grated zest of 1 lemon
pinch ground nutmeg

Fresh dairy ingredients are the heroes of this fabulous Yorkshire favourite. It's wonderful to make the pastry case yourself, but if you're short of time, you can use a shop-bought all-butter pastry case instead.

Sift the flour and salt into a large mixing bowl. Rub in the butter and vegetable fat with your fingertips until the mixture resembles fine breadcrumbs. Stir in the sweetener, then add enough chilled water to make a firm dough. Knead lightly for a few moments then wrap in clingfilm and refrigerate for about 10 minutes.

Preheat the oven to 200°C/400°F/gas mark 6.

Roll out the pastry on a lightly floured surface and use to line a 23cm pie plate or flan dish. Prick the base, line with tinfoil and bake blind (without the filling) for 10 minutes. Remove the tinfoil and cool slightly. Reduce the oven temperature to 180°C/350°F/gas mark 4.

For the filling, beat the eggs and single cream together in a mixing bowl. Add the cottage cheese, sweetener, vanilla extract, currants and lemon zest. Pour into the pastry case and sprinkle with the ground nutmeg.

Bake for 30–35 minutes, until the filling has set and turned a light golden brown. Serve warm.

Per serving: 308kcal; 10g protein; 17g fat; 8g saturated fat; 31g carbohydrates; 8.6g sugar; 1.1g fibre; 0.29g sodium

italian fruit trifle

SERVES 8

12 sponge fingers, broken in half

8 amaretti biscuits or 15 small ratafia
biscuits, lightly crushed

6 tablespoons marsala

250g strawberries, hulled and sliced

finely grated zest and juice of 2 oranges

2 tablespoons Splenda granulated
sweetener

250g blueberries

250g mascarpone cheese

142ml pot double cream

**This trifle is perfect for a dinner party – it's easy to whip up and your
guests will love the sensational flavours.**

Put the sponge fingers into the base of a trifle dish with most of the amaretti
or ratafia biscuits. Sprinkle evenly with the marsala, then scatter most of the
strawberries over the top.

Put the orange juice and sweetener into a saucepan and heat until simmering.
Add most of the blueberries and simmer gently for 1 minute. Remove from the
heat and cool, then spoon into the trifle dish.

Beat the mascarpone cheese until softened, then whisk in the cream and
orange zest. Spoon into the trifle dish, spreading it out to cover the fruit.

Decorate the trifle with the reserved biscuits, blueberries and strawberries.
Cover and refrigerate until ready to serve.

Per serving: 353kcal; 3g protein; 28g fat; 16.6g saturated fat; 21g carbohydrates;
14.7g sugar; 1.1g fibre; 0.08g sodium

little summer puddings

SERVES 4

225g blueberries
3 tablespoons Splenda granulated
   sweetener
150g strawberries, hulled and sliced
150g raspberries
6 slices medium-cut white bread

This delightful dessert helps you make the most of those delicious, fresh summer berries. Out of season, just thaw some frozen summer fruits instead.

Put the blueberries and sweetener into a saucepan with 1 tablespoon of cold water. Cook gently until juice just begins to run from the fruit – this will take about 2–3 minutes. Remove from the heat and add the strawberries and raspberries. Leave to cool.

Stamp out circles from the bread, using biscuit cutters, to fit into four individual pudding basins. You need four circles of about 5cm, four circles of about 6cm and four of about 7.5cm.

Put the small bread circles into the individual pudding basins. Divide half the fruit mixture over the basins. Layer the medium-sized bread circles on top, then spoon in the remaining fruit. Top with the large bread circles, then spoon any remaining fruit juice over. Cover with clingfilm and refrigerate for several hours, or overnight.

To serve, run a knife around the inside of each basin and turn out the puddings onto individual plates. Great served with single cream or yogurt.

Per serving: 200kcal; 6g protein; 1g fat; 0g saturated fat; 44g carbohydrates; 10.1g sugar; 3.4g fibre; 0.35g sodium

queen of puddings

SERVES 4

10g butter
75g fresh white breadcrumbs
450ml milk
½ teaspoon vanilla extract
3 tablespoons Splenda granulated
    sweetener
2 large eggs, separated
2 tablespoons raspberry jam

This classic British pudding is topped with a golden crown of meringue. Serve it straight from the oven.

Preheat the oven to 180°C/350°F/gas mark 4. Grease a 1.2 litre baking dish with a little of the butter. Sprinkle the breadcrumbs into the baking dish.

Heat the milk, remaining butter and vanilla extract until just lukewarm – take care that the mixture does not get too hot. Remove from the heat and add 2 tablespoons of the sweetener. Beat in the egg yolks. Pour into the baking dish, mix with the breadcrumbs, then leave to soak for 15–20 minutes.

Bake in the oven for 20–25 minutes, until set. Remove the baking dish from oven and cool slightly.

Whisk the egg whites in a grease-free bowl until they hold their shape, then add the remaining sweetener and whisk again until you have a thick, glossy meringue. Spread the jam over the surface of the pudding, then pile the meringue on top. Bake for a further 5–8 minutes, until golden brown.

Per serving: 208kcal; 10g protein; 8g fat; 3.3g saturated fat; 26g carbohydrates; 12.4g sugar; 0.4g fibre; 0.25g sodium

FAMILY FAVOURITES

hot and cold drinks

kiwi and raspberry smoothie

SERVES 2

4 kiwis

350g fresh, ripe raspberries

2 tablespoons yogurt

1 tablespoon Splenda granulated
  sweetener

Peel and roughly chop the kiwis. Place the raspberries, kiwis, yogurt and sweetener into a liquidiser and blitz until smooth.

Taste and adjust the sweetness as required. Chill in the refrigerator for 30 minutes and serve decorated with some extra raspberries or kiwi slices if you like.

Per serving: 62kcal; 3g protein; 1g fat; 0.1g saturated fat; 12g carbohydrates; 11.9g sugar; 3.3g fibre; 0.02g sodium

tropical fruit smoothie

SERVES 2

1 banana

100g strawberries

100g mango

1 papaya, peeled and thinly sliced

150ml orange juice

1 tablespoon runny honey

1 tablespoon Splenda granulated
  sweetener

1 tablespoon lemon juice

Peel the banana and slice in half lengthways. Hull the strawberries and cut them in half from top to tip. Peel, stone and cube the mango. Peel the papaya and scoop out the seeds, then slice the flesh.

Lay all the fruits on a small baking tray and freeze for about 2 hours until solid, but not deep-frozen.

Put the fruits into a liquidiser with the remaining ingredients and blitz to a purée. Pour into tall glasses and chill before serving.

Per serving: 186kcal; 2g protein; 1g fat; 0.1g saturated fat; 46g carbohydrates; 44.5g sugar; 5.2g fibre; 0.02g sodium

mexican hot chocolate

SERVES 4

500ml whole milk
150g Mexican chocolate, broken into
   pieces
½ tablespoon Splenda granulated
   sweetener

Mexico is the home of chocolate and has many varieties available. Good, dark, unsweetened chocolate can be melted into the most delicious of drinks – warming in winter and very moreish. Use the best quality chocolate you can find.

Put the milk and chocolate pieces into a large saucepan and add 500ml of water. Place over a low heat and stir until the chocolate is completely melted.

Continue to stir, bringing the mixture to almost simmering point. Keep it there for about 5 minutes to allow the flavours to develop.

Add the sweetener and stir in well, cooking the hot chocolate for a further minute. Remove from the heat and pour into a liquidiser. Blitz until frothy, then pour into four good-sized mugs. Now drink!

Per serving: 295kcal; 7g protein; 20g fat; 10.8g saturated fat; 23g carbohydrates; 16.5g sugar; 2.2g fibre; 0.05g sodium

sloe gin

MAKES 1.2 LITRES

850g sloes or bullaces
200g caster sugar
1.2 litres gin
6 tablespoons Splenda granulated
 sweetener

Sloe gin is best left for a year before drinking, if you can bear to, although it doesn't taste bad that first Christmas! You can make this with sloes, which taste very bitter, or with bullaces (wild plums found in the hedgerows) which are less tart and require less sweetening. Bullaces have a wonderful rich colour. This drink does need some sugar to develop the alcohol; however this version, with reduced sugar and added sweetener, works well too.

Wash the fruit and dry thoroughly. Prick in several places with a needle and put them into a sterilised glass jar (see page 76).

Add the sugar and pour in the gin. Seal the jar tightly and leave for 2–3 months, shaking every couple of days at first and when you remember later on. It will be ready to bottle then, at which time you should strain the gin, stir in the sweetener and bottle the liquid. The more it matures, the richer the flavours that develop, so try and leave it for another year.

Per 25ml serving: 76kcal; 0g protein; 0g fat; 0g saturated fat; 6g carbohydrates; 5.6g sugar; 0g fibre; 0g sodium

mulled wine

SERVES 8

1 bottle dry red wine

5 tablespoons Splenda granulated
  sweetener

125ml brandy

2 cinnamon sticks

6 whole cloves

pinch of grated nutmeg

2 oranges, thinly sliced

1 lemon, thinly sliced

Variations of this drink can be found around the world, from Sweden to Germany, from Moldova to Mexico. It's a warming drink, perfect at a cold Bonfire Night party.

Place the red wine, sweetener, brandy, cinnamon, cloves, nutmeg and citrus fruit into a large, heavy pan. Add 125ml of water, place on a low heat and gently bring to a simmer, stirring occasionally to bruise the fruit. Once the sweetener is dissolved and the mixture fragrant, remove from the heat and serve.

Per serving: 111kcal; 0g protein; 0g fat; 0g saturated fat; 3g carbohydrates; 2.8g sugar; 0.3g fibre; 0.01g sodium

elderflower syrup

MAKES ABOUT 1.25 LITRES

6 tablespoons Splenda granulated
  sweetener

12 elderflower heads

4 unwaxed lemons

Place a heavy-based saucepan with 1.25 litres of cold water on a medium heat and dissolve the sweetener. Gently stir in the elderflower heads with a wooden spoon. Bring the liquid to the boil and cook for about 5 minutes. Meanwhile, grate the zest from the lemons and then squeeze out the juice. Add to the pan and stir well. Continue to boil for a further 1 minute, then remove the pan from the heat. Leave to cool and infuse for 24 hours.

Strain the mixture through a muslin cloth and bottle it. Store in a cool place – it should keep for 1–2 months. Dilute to the strength required.

Per 30ml serving: 11kcal; 0g protein; 0g fat; 0g saturated fat; 3g carbohydrates; 2.8g sugar; 0g fibre; 0g sodium

sweet geranium leaf lemonade

SERVES 6

2 large handfuls of young sweet
   geranium leaves
8 tablespoons Splenda granulated
   sweetener
juice of 3 unwaxed lemons
about 800ml sparkling water

Sweet geraniums (*Pelargonium graveolens)* have divinely fragrant leaves and flower in summer. There are many different varieties from the delicately pink-flowered *Pelargonium* 'Attar of Roses' to the white-flowered *Pelargonium odoratissimum*. The Victorians loved them! They make a magnificent flavoured lemonade with a difference.

Hold the sweet geranium leaves over a big, stainless steel pan. Crush them in your fist to bruise them slightly – this will bring out the scent – and drop them into the pan.

Add the sweetener and 600ml of tap water and heat gently and slowly. Bring the water just to boiling point and simmer for 3 minutes or so. Remove from the heat, stir in the lemon juice and leave to cool.

When cold, dilute with sparkling water to taste. Chill and serve with ice cubes.

Per serving: 62kcal; 0g protein; 0g fat; 0g saturated fat; 17g carbohydrates; 16.3g sugar; 0g fibre; 0g sodium

strawberry squash

SERVES 2

225g ripe strawberries, hulled
2 tablespoons Splenda granulated
 sweetener
juice of ½ lemon, strained

This is a truly refreshing recipe which makes a change from lemonade on hot summer days. Pick the strawberries when they are really ripe and red all over – this squash will taste so much better for it!

Place the strawberries and sweetener in a liquidiser with 150ml of water and blitz to a purée.

Pass the purée through a fine sieve and place it in a jelly bag suspended over a bowl. Leave to drip through and, when the pulp in the jelly bag is dry, add another 300ml of water and allow this to drip through as well.

Mix in the strained lemon juice and dilute with iced water to taste.

Per serving: 36kcal; 1g protein; 0g fat; 0g saturated fat; 8g carbohydrates; 8.4g sugar; 1.2g fibre; 0.01g sodium

bonfire night punch

SERVES 10

6 large Bramley apples, unpeeled, cored
  and diced
1 litre cider
1 tablespoon Splenda granulated
  sweetener
3 cinnamon sticks
3 star anise
250ml dark rum

**This rum and cider punch is hugely comforting to drink whilst your
children run around the bonfire. It goes well with a good slab of porter
cake (see page 68) and is best made 24 hours before serving so that
the flavours really do get the chance to mingle. Use strong cider and
good-quality Bramley apples if you can.**

Put the apples, cider, sweetener, cinnamon sticks and star anise into a large
pan. Add 1 litre of water and bring just to the boil, stirring well. Turn the heat
down and simmer for 1 hour and 15 minutes.

Pour in the rum and continue to cook for 1 minute or so. Remove from the heat
and set aside to cool. Serve either warm or cold – just make sure the mixture
doesn't come to the boil when you reheat it.

Per serving: 134kcal; 0g protein; 0g fat; 0g saturated fat; 13g carbohydrates;
13.4g sugar; 1.6g fibre; 0.01g sodium

christmas punch

SERVES 15

3 bottles red wine
4 tablespoons Splenda granulated
   sweetener
3 cloves
pinch of nutmeg
1–1½ cinnamon sticks
300ml dark rum
zest and juice of 1 lemon
zest and juice of 3 oranges

Melinda says: Christmas just wouldn't be the same without this delicious drink. It fully embodies the spirit of Christmas – just don't drink too much!

Put the red wine, sweetener, cloves, nutmeg, cinnamon sticks, rum, lemon and orange zest into a large, stainless steel saucepan. Warm it gently until it just reaches simmering point, then add the lemon and orange juice. Continue cooking for a couple of minutes, then leave to cool slightly and serve in tall tumblers.

Per serving: 153kcal; 0g protein; 0g fat; 0g saturated fat; 2g carbohydrates; 1.9g sugar; 0g fibre; 0.01g sodium

conversion chart

Weight (solids)

7g	¼oz	375g	13oz
10g	½oz	400g	14oz
20g	¾oz	425g	15oz
25g	1oz	450g	1lb
40g	1½oz	500g (½kg)	18oz
50g	2oz	600g	1¼lb
60g	2½oz	700g	1½lb
75g	3oz	750g	1lb 10oz
100g	3½oz	900g	2lb
110g	4oz (¼lb)	1kg	2¼lb
125g	4½oz	1.1kg	2½lb
150g	5½oz	1.2kg	2lb 12oz
175g	6oz	1.3kg	3lb
200g	7oz	1.5kg	3lb 5oz
225g	8oz (½lb)	1.6kg	3½lb
250g	9oz	1.8kg	4lb
275g	10oz	2kg	4lb 8oz
300g	10½oz	2.25kg	5lb
310g	11oz	2.5kg	5lb 8oz
325g	11½oz	3kg	6lb 8oz
350g	12oz (¾lb)		

Volume (liquids)

5ml	1 teaspoon
10ml	1 dessertspoon
15ml	1 tablespoon or
	½fl oz
30ml	1fl oz
40ml	1½fl oz
50ml	2fl oz
60ml	2½fl oz
75ml	3fl oz
100ml	3½fl oz
125ml	4fl oz
150ml	5fl oz (¼ pint)
160ml	5½fl oz
175ml	6fl oz
200ml	7fl oz
225ml	8fl oz
250ml (0.25 litre)	9fl oz
300ml	10fl oz (½ pint)
325ml	11fl oz
350ml	12fl oz
370ml	13fl oz
400ml	14fl oz
425ml	15fl oz (¾ pint)
450ml	16fl oz
500ml (0.5 litre)	18fl oz
550ml	19fl oz
600ml	20fl oz (1 pint)
700ml	1¼ pints
850ml	1½ pints
1 litre	1¾ pints
1.2 litres	2 pints
1.5 litres	2½ pints
1.8 litres	3 pints
2 litres	3½ pints

Length

5mm	¼ inch
1cm	½ inch
2cm	¾ inch
2.5cm	1 inch
3cm	1¼ inches
4cm	1½ inches
5cm	2 inches
7.5 cm	3 inches
10cm	4 inches
15cm	6 inches
18cm	7 inches
20cm	8 inches
24cm	10 inches
28cm	11 inches
30 cm	12 inches

Oven temperatures

110°C/225°F/gas mark ½	cool
120°C/250°F/gas mark ½	cool
130°C/275°F/gas mark 1	very low
150°C/300°F/gas mark 2	very low
160°C/325°F/gas mark 3	low
180°C/350°F/gas mark 4	moderate
190°C/375°F/gas mark 5	moderately hot
200°C/400°F/gas mark 6	hot
220°C/425°F/gas mark 7	hot
230°C/450°F/gas mark 8	very hot
240°C/475°F/gas mark 9	very hot

For fan-assisted ovens, reduce temperatures by 10°C

Temperature conversion

°C=5/9 (°F-32)

°F=9/5 °C+32

index